Construction and Testing of Theories in Sociology

A Primer on the Construction and Testing of Theories in Sociology

JANET SALTZMAN CHAFETZ

University of Houston

F. E. PEACOCK PUBLISHERS, INC.

ITASCA, ILLINOIS 60143

Preface

This book is written primarily for undergraduate sociology majors with no background in sociological theory, methods, or philosophy. Although it presupposes some exposure to sociology, generally a student who has taken no more than an introductory course should have sufficient background to read this book. This primer emerges from my own need for appropriate reading material to assign students struggling to gain a rudimentary understanding of what might generally be termed "the philosophy of social science." Almost all sociology departments require undergraduate majors to study "theory" and "methods." Many professors are concerned with relating the two areas to one another, demonstrating how theory informs research and vice versa, as well as the necessity for both endeavors in the development of the field. However, extant books in the area have not, by and large, been pitched to the comprehension of undergraduates, especially those lacking background in the three areas mentioned above. I think that undergraduate students are able to grasp the central ideas of the philosophy of social science when they are presented in simple language with everyday examples. Moreover, in the exercise of learning this material students develop more precision of thought, sharpening their analytical and synthesizing skills. I strongly believe that the development of these intellectual attributes stands at the core of a liberal education and is desirable whether or not students later become professional social scientists.

It is my hope that this primer is simple enough to be readily comprehensible by undergraduates without simplifying to the point of inaccuracy. Most of the details and subtle distinctions involved in the

v

philosophy of science are ignored, since they are well covered in a variety of more advanced books. It is further hoped that, given the relative brevity of this primer, it will better enable teachers to incorporate at least a brief unit on the philosophy of social science into their theory and/or methods courses at the undergraduate level.

I wish to thank Helen Rose Ebaugh, David Bell, Henry Chafetz, Rosalind Dworkin, and Anthony Gary Dworkin for their helpful comments on an earlier draft of this manuscript. I also thank Arlene Thomas for secretarial assistance. I am especially indebted to my former mentor, Joseph Lopreato, for introducing me to the challenge of theory and to the rigors of theory construction while I was still a neophyte in sociology.

Houston, Texas
September 1977

JANET SALTZMAN CHAFETZ

Contents

CHAPTER 1

The Role of Theory
in Sociology

True   False   Check the correct column for each of the following:

——— ———   1. Theories are speculations about things you're not sure of.

——— ———   2. Theories are statements about facts you are sure of.

——— ———   3. Theories in sociology are no more or less than the writings of the discipline's early founders, such as Marx, Comte, Weber, Durkheim.

——— ———   4. Theories are mathematical statements.

——— ———   5. The word "theory" is synonymous with the term "scientific laws."

——— ———   6. The word "theory" is synonymous with the word "classification."

——— ———   7. Theories are the verbal form of correlations and other statistics.

——— ———   8. The word "theory" means the same thing as the word "prediction."

——— ———   9. Theories in sociology are mostly concerned with answering the questions of when and where something has happened and/or will happen.

1

True   False

_____	_____	10.	Theories are sets of definitions.
_____	_____	11.	At least a few theories have been proven to be true, even if none of these are sociological theories.
_____	_____	12.	Theories and assumptions are the same things.
_____	_____	13.	I'm not sure what a theory is.

If you answered the first twelve questions above "false," you may be correct in answering number 13 in the same fashion. If, however, you said that any of the first 12 assertions was true, then you are indeed not sure what theories are, for the correct answers to the statements, as worded, are all "false." Before exploring further these common misunderstandings of the nature of theory, a brief definition of what theories are in all scientific disciplines is in order: *Theories consist of a series of relatively abstract and general statements which collectively purport to explain (answer the question "why?") some aspect of the empirical world (the "reality" known to us directly or indirectly through our senses).* The elements of this definition are simple. Once something is established as existing, theories constitute systematic attempts to answer the general question "why?"

In a simple, more or less unconscious sense, we are all constantly engaged in theorizing in our everyday life. If, for instance, an old friend did something totally out of keeping with her or his typical or anticipated behavior, you would be likely to ask yourself "why?" You would then mentally review several alternative explanations (emotional strain, unusual situation, you never really understood the person in the first place, maturation, etc.) and, for various reasons, reject some or most of them. You might eventually settle upon one reason and elaborate the details further. The mental exercise of theory construction is not basically different from this everyday experience. In theory construction, the exercise is only more systematic, more comprehensive, more guided and constrained by rules, and finally, more self-conscious. This book will spell out some of the ways by which one can make this everyday exercise more systematic, comprehensive and self-conscious.

A. WHAT THEORIES ARE NOT (BUT ARE OFTEN THOUGHT TO BE)

Statements 1, 2, and 12 at the beginning of this chapter all address the same misunderstanding conveyed by the often heard remark "that's not fact, it's only a theory." The words "fact" and "theory," however, are not opposites. Through empirical research an attempt is made to establish the facts of a situation. Theorizing occurs when an attempt is made to explain why the facts are as they are. Of course, research and theorizing are interrelated processes which constantly inform each other. The relationship between the two will be discussed throughout this book. For now, however, it is sufficient to note that the words "fact" and "theory" refer to completely different phenomena and therefore cannot be opposites. It is a fact that many people live in places we call cities. We attempt to explain that fact with reference to a number of psychological, economic, political, and cultural reasons, chosen on the basis of the facts we know about them. The explanations themselves, however, are imputed by the human mind to account for the facts we observe and can thus never be proven true. We can demonstrate, for instance, that people move to cities where jobs exist. However, it is we who say that the availability of jobs is what causes people to move. We can pile up evidence that cumulatively adds weight to our explanations of the facts, but it is always potentially or logically possible that the very next time we examine reality, something will appear that contradicts our explanation. Thus, for instance, the next time we look we may find people moving to cities where there are no available jobs. Thus, while the facts may show a theory to be false, it can never be said conclusively that a theory is true. For this reason, statement 11 is false.

Statements 6, 9, and 10 are incorrect by definition. We shall see later that theories contain definitions and often classifications, but these things are components of, not themselves, explanations. Moreover, theories attempt to answer the question "why?" but not necessarily "where?" or "when?" Explanation of why something exists or occurs may or may not enable one to predict when or where it will happen again. In a laboratory situation where the various factors thought to cause something to happen can be controlled, prediction typically results from explanation. In real-life settings, as will be explained further in the next chapter, predictions (and thus the answers to "when?" and/or "where?") are often impossible. Thus, statement 8 is false.

Theories in some sciences, such as physics, are normally stated in the form of mathematical equations. Mathematics itself is neither more nor less than a highly precise system of general symbols, namely, a language. Theories may be stated in any language, thus statement 4 is false.

3

However, the more precise the language the better suited it is for purposes of theory construction and testing.

Theories consist of statements called propositions (see Chapter 6) which, if widely agreed upon and heavily supported by research findings, are sometimes called "scientific laws." However, theories also consist of definitions and assumptions, as well as a series of several propositions only some or none of which may be sufficiently well supported to be termed "laws." Therefore, it is not true to say, as statement 5 does, that theories and scientific laws are one and the same thing.

Testing theories in sociology often involves the use of correlations and other statistical procedures. These techniques aid in the discovery of facts. A correlation coefficient, for instance, tells us to what extent two or more variables are related to one another. Stated simply, it tells us to what extent one thing occurs when something else does or does not occur. This is not, however, an explanation; the question of why the two phenomena are (or are not) related to one another is not answered by that statistic or any other. The human mind, not a statistical formula, has to attempt to provide the link that answers "why?" Thus, statement 7 is false; theories are not a verbal form of statistics.

The final misconception about the nature of theory is embodied in statement 3. Sociology "theory courses" are often no more or less than the intellectual history of the discipline. They may be broadly inclusive and, beginning with Comte (or occasionally even with earlier social philosophers), cover a large number of relatively famous sociologists (most if not all of whom are long deceased). They may be more narrow in scope, concentrating on the sociological giants (Marx, Durkheim, Weber, Parsons, Merton, Simmel, Pareto). The student reads literature (primary and/or secondary) rich in definitions, classifications, brilliant insights, outrageously incorrect predictions, vague speculations, debates over what sociology ought to study and the appropriate methods for such study, and penetrating analyses of a large variety of social, cultural and social-psychological phenomena. Furthermore, the student typically learns that Durkheim was influenced by Comte; that Weber was responding to the "ghost of Marx"; that Parsons introduced Weber to sociology in the United States—in short, the student learns about the historical continuities and discontinuities in the development of the discipline.

While I do not mean to denigrate the importance of this type of

4

learning, I do wish to argue that theory and intellectual history are not the same thing. The primary reason for sociologists (as contrasted with historians) to read the works of our intellectual forebears is to cull out of their works those insights which are relevant to our work today, namely, understanding and explaining social and social-psychological phenomena as they can be demonstrated to exist empirically. Stated in another way, we read Marx or Weber or Parsons not primarily to understand Marx or Weber or Parsons but to understand the world as we can know it "factually." The brilliance of these scholars as social thinkers and observers helps in that understanding. However, that help is contingent upon sorting out the brilliant insights and analyses from the rest of the verbiage and subsequently rendering this residue into a format that is useful for research and explanation. That format is theory, the various components of which you will be learning throughout this primer.

B. Levels of Abstraction

The empirical world is comprised of almost infinite variety. Each book is different in some one or more ways from all other books; each family from all others, and so on. To make sense out of the barrage of sensory inputs to which all people are constantly exposed, humans abstract certain common elements from a number of concrete cases and are thus able to identify particular cases as part of a class of objects. Thus, the word "book" is an abstraction which concentrates attention on a physical object with covers, between which a sheaf of papers is bound, each paper in turn containing symbols, pictures, and/or illustrations, and so forth. We systematically ignore differences in size, color, number of pages, type of printing and so on in conceptualizing the general word "book."

All words and concepts are, to some degree, abstractions. Words vary along a continuum in their degree of abstractness, however. Toward one extreme are words such as "book" which conjure up a fairly concrete image in the mind. If you close your eyes you can visualize "a book." At the other extreme there are highly abstract words which refer to a wide range of concrete phenomena that vary in a multitude of ways and may have only one or two common elements. You cannot readily close your eyes and envision "democracy," "social status," or "social system."

It is important to understand that in any science the terms employed

5

CONSTRUCTION AND TESTING OF THEORIES

vary all along this continuum of abstractness. Thus, for instance, the concept "crime" is more concrete than the term "deviance," which includes crimes but also other forms of norm or rule breaking. In turn, "crime" is a more abstract term than "rape" or "burglary," both of which, along with many other legal infractions, are subsumed by the more abstract terms.

The scientific process involves the ability to move back and forth along the continuum of abstractness. When engaged in fact gathering, one is working at the relatively concrete or less abstract end of the continuum. In interpreting the results of a research project, one moves toward the middle of the continuum. In theorizing one is working with higher levels of abstraction. Theory and research inform one another, as we shall see more clearly later, and therefore, words and concepts of differing degrees of abstractness must be carefully related to one another in the same way that the terms "rape," "crime," and "deviance" are interrelated.

Much of what has been called "theory" in sociology has consisted of terms that are so highly abstract and general that researchers find it difficult if not impossible to relate the theory to the concrete world. For instance, the Structural-Functional school of social theory uses extremely abstract language as does the recent approach known as Phenomenology. Such "theory," therefore, fails in its essential function of helping to explain that which we know about empirical reality. In response to this situation the contemporary sociologist, Robert K. Merton (1957, p. 9), has called for the development of *theories of the middle range.* Merton asks sociologists to be more modest in their goals when developing theories. Instead of attempting to develop highly general and, therefore, abstract theories to explain the structure and functioning of total societies, he proposes that *a series of less general theories be developed to explain smaller components of social reality.* Thus, Merton's approach would have sociologists concentrate on developing theories of deviance, stratification, minority-majority relations, population change, and so forth that are less abstract but more closely tied to empirical reality, thus more testable. Only after a number of such theories are developed should attempts be made to move up in level of abstraction and develop more general, all-encompassing theories. To use an analogy, Merton is telling the discipline to develop a Newtonian theory of mechanics before it attempts an Einsteinian theory of relativity.

6

In this book the word "theory" will be used largely as Merton suggested. The approaches and considerations discussed will emphasize the need constantly to relate theory to research, abstract explanation to concrete reality. Thus, the student will need to become comfortable in moving back and forth along the continuum of abstractness.

C. WHERE DO THEORIES COME FROM?

The simplest answer to this question is anywhere and everywhere. Theories can start from a hunch, from a personal experience, from reading what other scholars have said, from an exercise in pure logic, from an insight derived from a movie, a play, a novel. No matter what the source of inspiration, all theories develop ultimately through the interrelated use of two processes: inductive logic and deductive logic.

Inductive logic may be defined as reasoning from the concrete or specific to the general (i.e., from less to more abstractness). *Deductive logic is the opposite: reasoning from the general or abstract to the specific or concrete.* The first stage of theory construction may be either inductive or deductive, but whichever it is, the next stage will be the opposite, and further development will involve movement back and forth between the two. The rules of logic are used in this process, which also involves research. For instance, a relatively abstract theory is analyzed in terms of how it may be converted into a series of statements pertaining more directly to the concrete world. This is the process of deduction. These concrete statements are then tested through research. The results of the research are then examined and related logically to the abstract theory, often resulting in change or revision of the original theory (see Chapter 7). At this point, induction is being employed. The revised, expanded, new, or even same theory will subsequently be subjected to further testing, and so on in a process that is fundamentally endless. Conversely, one could begin with a series of findings and induce a general explanation. Deduction would then be employed to retranslate this explanation into statements which are amenable to further research, and so on.

Let us suppose that we have created a theory to explain why people commit acts defined as socially deviant. Our theory claims that people become deviant because they associate with other deviants and thus learn their deviance in the same way people generally learn conformity. We decide that one test of this theory involves those acts of deviance we call "crime" and, further, that the particular manifestations of crime with which we are concerned are muggings, burglaries, and embezzlement. We decide that association with other deviants is manifested by the number of friends a person has who have been arrested for the same types of crimes. We have, to this point, been engaged in deduction. We then do research to see if indeed people who commit the three types of crimes have more friends who have also committed these crimes, when compared with people who have not committed these crimes. Let us further suppose that the results of the research support our assertion, but only for males, not for females. We now become involved in induction as we correct our theory to account for the observed difference between the two sexes. We would then return to the deductive approach and subsequently test our revised theory. We might do so by using a different set of observable manifestations of either or both concepts. For instance, "deviance" might be observed by using different types of crimes or evidence of the breaking of certain social (but not legal) conventions.

This process comes into play only when someone has been sufficiently creative to begin the tentative development of a theory. In one sense, imagination and creativity cannot be taught in a textbook; only the means by which they may be channeled and developed are amenable to rules and guidelines. However, there are mechanisms that increase the likelihood that someone will stumble upon a creative insight that can be subsequently developed into a theory. For most professional social scientists the starting point is typically reading widely and critically what others, past and present, have had to say about some phenomenon. Such reading is often called a "literature search," and it may alert the careful reader to phenomena lacking an explanation, to explanations contradicted by some set of facts, to contradictions between two or more different theories, and so forth. There is no substitute for a thorough knowledge of the work done previously on a subject, even if all one learns from that reading is that we are collectively ignorant about something. At the very least, it prevents us from wasting time and resources exploring the same dead ends already explored by others.

However, science and theory do not simply build cumulatively as one scientist's work inspires another. Often serendipity—or plain luck— plays a crucial role in theory development. It may be that in the process of researching something, a fact, often unrelated to the original purpose of the research, is discovered that sets thinking in a new direction. It may

8

be that a movie, novel, poem, or personal discussion or experience sets off a chain of thought or provides an insight that becomes the germ of a theory. But these accidental happenings are unlikely to be perceived as relevant to theory building if one does not already possess the intellectual tools and background knowledge to recognize their importance and/or newness. One can only take advantage of "luck" if one has the necessary skills and background to do so. Thus, once again we are back to the irreplaceable role of reading widely, carefully, and critically what others have said about a subject.

D. WHAT ARE THEORIES USED FOR?

The United States has long been known as a very pragmatic or practical society and culture. We Americans tend to ask of a new idea or development "What is it good for?" "To what practical use can we put it?" Yet, we are also heir to a long cultural tradition, dating back many centuries to our (generally) European cultural roots, which values knowledge and learning for its own sake, for no end beyond the satisfaction of intellectual curiosity, as a goal or end in its own right.

Many scientists, irrespective of their particular field of interest, and especially those who work in college or university settings rather than in industry or government, have intellectual curiosity as their primary motivation. They seek knowledge in order to satisfy that curiosity, whether or not any practical benefits result from the effort. This is one reason why academicians are sometimes viewed as existing in an "ivory tower" or in a world that is rather remote from the everyday experience of the rest of the society. In their never-ending quest to gain new knowledge, scientists sometimes study things that appear trivial or impractical to others.

The first "use" of theory, then, is not a "use" at all in the practical sense of the word. Theory helps to satisfy intellectual curiosity, a trait that is, at least to some extent, often considered in the Western world as a major hallmark of our species. However, the money that supports scientists and scientific enterprise (which is indeed a very costly undertaking) comes largely from government and industry, namely, from people and institutions which are interested in the practical utility of scientific discovery. Moreover, in many sciences, including sociology, a substantial proportion of practitioners have practical motives which guide their work. For instance, many sociologists explicitly wish to understand their society better in order to change it in some manner, to alleviate social problems, to help the disadvantaged and powerless.

Theories help us to understand why things occur as they do. Thus, sooner or later most theories can have practical utility for someone. If, for instance, a school board wishes to increase the reading level of urban children, a clear understanding of why they read poorly can help in identifying workable strategies for improvement. Sometimes, however, the reasons why something occurs are precisely those phenomena which are least amenable to outside intervention, and thus understanding cannot lead to practical steps toward change. If those children read poorly because they are allowed to watch too much television and thus never practice reading outside the classroom, there is little the school board can do to directly rectify the situation. However, if their reading is poor because they are bored with their texts, then the school board can remedy the situation by ordering different, more interesting reading material.

Theories—indeed all knowledge—are double-edged swords, and serious ethical problems thus underlie their development. The same theory that brought us nuclear energy for use in generating electricity and in many medical cures brought us nuclear weapons and nuclear contamination; cellular theories that may eventually help to eradicate cancer may also be misused to create genetic "monsters"; the germ theory of disease brought preventive inoculations and the possibility of germ warfare; theories of behavior modification, helpful in training the mentally retarded to live a more independent and nearly "normal" life, can also be used to change involuntarily the personalities of those defined as social deviants or misfits, thereby infringing on their civil rights and liberties. The scientists who develop theories rarely have much say about how people, and especially the powerful few, will utilize them in practical application. Theories may be used for good or for evil. Indeed, it is likely that theories which are powerful enough to eventuate in massive good are likewise powerful enough to result in massive bad if used by unscrupulous, unethical, careless, ignorant, short-sighted, or stupid human beings.

Theories also can be used practically through the related creation of simulations and games. Simulations, often done on computers, attempt to create a model of a real-life situation and, by varying certain inputs, see what happens as a result. Thus, the potential effects of a given plan of action, event, etc., may be anticipated before it is tried on living human beings and/or before the occasion demands its use. Simulations are usually grounded in theories. Thus, for instance, a theory about how people react to natural disasters, plus factual data about transportation routes, population numbers, residential patterns, and so forth may be expressed as a simulation of what would happen if a severe earthquake struck San Francisco. From the results of the simulation, plans could be created to help reduce or alleviate certain types of problems if the earthquake were to occur.

Games are similar to simulations in that they are theory-based models of real behavior. However, they are played by people who assume various roles in a predefined, rule-bound situation, and there are usually winners and losers. Games are primarily used as pedagogical techniques to teach students something about the "real world" when it is not possible or practical for them to learn by first-hand experience. There are games which teach students to function as lobbyists and politicians within our political system, corporate executives, and so forth.

The final, major use of theory is as a guide to research. There is virtually an infinite number of phenomena one could potentially research; there is essentially an infinite number of facts to be discovered about our physical and social world. Collection of mere facts without some organizing framework is not only never-ending but meaningless. To assimilate mentally, use, understand, or indeed do anything beyond collect them, facts must be organized somehow. One very important way to decide what facts to seek and how to understand them once collected is to employ some theory as the basic organizational principle. Using deductive logic, theory serves as a guide to defining the realm of facts to be collected. Inductive logic will subsequently enable the researcher to interpret better the meaning of those facts. Common sense notwithstanding, facts never "speak for themselves"; they are always recognized as worthy of notice and understood within some interpretive framework. One person may dismiss something because "*only* one-third of all people in this country ever do x"; a different person, appraised of the same "fact," may proclaim the importance of this phenomenon with "It's astounding; one in three people do x!" Indeed, some "facts" are totally ignored, not recognized as "facts," until a new theory suggests that they are worthy of note. Thus, our theories both blind us to some things that they define as irrelevant and alert us to others so that we may perceive and better comprehend them. Without the "selective perception" or perceptual screen imposed by theories we would not see more; we would be effectively sightless. In short, theories help us to frame the questions we wish to ask of the world, to identify what is needed in order to answer those questions, and to understand the meaning of the facts our research efforts produce. Without theory there is no science, no intellectual comprehension of the world, only a mechanical, robotlike collection of random bits and pieces of reality. One might just as well collect bottle caps.

E. EXEMPLAR

In order to understand better the ways in which theories are developed in sociology, a single, somewhat simplified, middle-range theory will be developed in this book. Each chapter will end with a further step in the creation of this theory. It should be understood, however, that this material is presented as an example to aid in learning. The theory is still in the process of being developed and has not been tested systematically. Therefore, it should not be viewed as an accepted sociological theory. Two colleagues, Rosalind Dworkin and Anthony Gary Dworkin, and I have collectively developed these ideas over a two-year period. The theory presented in this book is a simplification of a somewhat more detailed work which is still in progress (Chafetz, Dworkin, and Dworkin, 1976).

It has been widely observed and reported in the sociological literature that, relative to white males, females and nonwhites in the United States share two characteristics: 1) They are less frequently employed in full-time jobs; and 2) Among the employed, women and nonwhites generally hold different, and typically less prestigious, more poorly paid jobs than white males. Moreover, over time the proportion of these groups employed full time varies, as does the degree to which they hold jobs similar to those held by white males. These well-established facts led us to ask "why?" Under what conditions are nonwhites and females (social minority groups) employed more fully? Under what conditions are they employed in the same kinds of occupations as white males (the social majority group)?

The existing literature contained many scattered insights and facts, but nowhere did we find a comprehensive statement concerning both racial-ethnic minorities and women. Moreover, nowhere were all the scattered reasons pulled together in one, more comprehensive theory. We set as our task the development of such a middle-range theory. We

12

thus began by employing inductive logic, attempting to move from a set of established facts reported in the literature to a general theory.

We were motivated in this endeavor by both intellectual curiosity and by more practical and personal concerns. If, in the process of developing this theory, we could identify factors which strongly influence the rate of group labor force participation and occupational deployment (i.e., what groups have what types of jobs), *and* find some which are amenable to public policy intervention, then we might contribute to changes which would enhance the job opportunities of nonwhites and females. In short, we hoped that our work might contribute in practical ways to achieving our nation's goal of equal employment opportunity. As recipients of past job discrimination and/or as friends of others who had experienced such problems, our commitment was highly personal as well.

In the remaining chapters you will see how this theory was developed. It should be noted, however, that the exact chronology of our work was not always the same as the order in which it is presented here. Constructing and testing theories rarely if ever occurs in the neat sequences presented by texts for the sake of clarity.

STUDENT EXERCISES

1. Think of some bit of behavior performed by a friend or relative that you recently observed and found unusual. List at least three possible explanations for the behavior. Review the "facts" in support of each possible explanation and those which contradict that explanation. What additional facts do you need to help you decide which, if any, are the best explanations?
2. For each of the following find a word or term which is more abstract but also encompasses the word given:
   a. Law
   b. Catholicism
   c. Corporation
   d. Mother
   e. Riot
3. For each of the following find a word or term which is less abstract but is also encompassed by the word given:
   a. Relative
   b. Mass media
   c. Subculture
   d. Institution
   e. Conflict

4. What are the chief reasons why you are interested in studying sociology? How do you think these reasons affect your particular interests, that is, the topics you most like to study in sociology?
5. Choose some phenomenon of sociological relevance for which you would like an explanation. State the issue precisely. Find a text for that specialty area and see if there are any existing theories that explain it. If there are, read the theory now, then reread it *critically* after you finish this primer. If there are not, speculate on an explanation and work on it again after you finish this primer.

CHAPTER 2

The Nature of Explanation

Theories are systems of explanation; they help to answer the question "why?" How, then, are answers to the questions "why?" developed and structured? This chapter attempts to provide answers to this question.

A. WHAT EXPLANATIONS ARE NOT (BUT ARE OFTEN THOUGHT TO BE)

In the last chapter one of the erroneous notions about theories offered stated that "Theories are the verbal form of correlations and other statistics." *A correlation coefficient is a statistic that tells us to what extent and in what way two variables are related to one another.* A positive sign on the correlation means that, as the value of one thing increases or decreases (e.g., income) so does the value of another (e.g., occupational prestige). This is called a *direct relationship.* The higher the income the higher the occupation prestige. A negative sign on the correlation tells us that as the value of something increases or decreases (e.g., proportion voting for the Republican party) the value of something else (proportion of people below the poverty level) goes in the opposite direction. This is called an *inverse relationship.* The greater the proportion of those in a precinct voting Republican, the fewer in that precinct fall below the poverty level. A correlation that approximates

15

CHART 2.1
Graphic Examples of Hypothetical Correlations

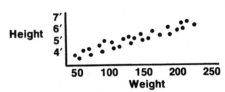

A high direct correlation. The hypothetical heights and weights of a sample of people are presented showing that the taller people are, the more they weigh. (approximately +.850)

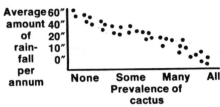

A high, inverse correlation. The hypothetical annual average rainfall amounts and prevalence of cactus for a sample of geographic areas are presented showing that the more the rainfall the less prevalent are cactus. (approximately −.850)

A moderate, direct correlation. The hypothetical educational levels and occupational prestige scores of a sample of people are presented showing a tendency for people with a lot of education to hold high prestige occupations. (approximately +.350)

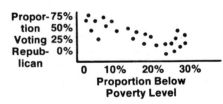

A moderate, inverse correlation. The hypothetical proportions of people below the poverty level and percent voting Republican in a sample of precincts are presented showing a tendency for precincts with a heavy Republican vote to have few poverty people. (approximately −.350)

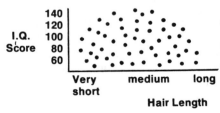

A zero correlation. The hypothetical I.Q. scores and hair lengths of a sample of people are presented showing no relationship between the two. (approximately .000)

16

zero tells us that no relationship appears to exist between the two phenomena (e.g., the proportion of students with brown eyes and the proportion of students planning to attend college). The numerical value of correlations can go only as high as 1.000. The range thus goes from +1.000, through zero, to -1.000. The strength of the relationship between the variables is signified by the numerical value of the correlation. For instance, a +.825 correlation, compared to a +.325, means that the two variables in the former case are more closely related than in the latter; in both cases the variables are directly related. Chart 2.1 depicts the various possibilities of linear (straight-line) relationships. More complex relationships, those which form various curves, are also possible, but they are beyond the scope of this primer.

As mentioned in the last chapter, correlations are not explanations. However, explanations always imply a relationship between variables and thus some form of correlation. Whenever you say something causes something else, it is logically necessary that they vary together, although they may vary inversely or directly, in a linear or a curvilinear fashion. Failure to find a correlation means that the explanation offered is incorrect (assuming that the research is not faulty). For instance, suppose we have a theory which says that boys run faster than girls because the former get more exercise than the latter. If our research shows no correlation between the amount of exercise a child gets and his or her running speed, then our explanation is wrong. However, what is more important, even high correlations in the expected direction do not conclusively prove the explanation; at most we have some additional support for an explanation. The statement of correlation per se is no more or less than a statement that X and Y are found together, *not why*. In short, a lack of a correlation can serve to disprove an explanation; its presence is not an explanation nor can it prove an explanation.

The primary reason why correlations cannot be used to prove an explanation is the possibility that the relationship noted may be spurious. *A spurious relationship occurs when an unknown third (fourth, fifth, etc.) element is systematically related to the two in question and provides the real link between the phenomena in question.* Let us suppose that during our research we discover a high, inverse correlation between the frequency with which children watch television and grades in school: the more TV children watch the lower their academic performance. Further, other data show that extensive TV viewing is highly correlated with failure to practice reading at home and failure to

17

complete homework assignments. From this we develop an explanation that directly links TV viewing to academic achievement by arguing that TV detracts from the time that should be spent reading and doing homework and thus results in low grades. However, there are other possibilities which could make this linkage spurious. For instance, maybe the type of parents who permit extensive TV viewing are the same type who neither encourage nor reward academic achievement. If this were the case, it might be parental lack of support for academic achievement which explains student failure to practice reading or complete homework and ultimately low grades, not TV watching per se. Something about parental values and/or behaviors might explain both phenomena in question, which may not themselves be directly linked.

There is one final reason why correlations are not the same thing as explanations. All a correlation tells us is that two things vary either directly or inversely; it does not tell us which of the two has impact on the other. For instance, there is a fairly high, positive correlation among adults between educational level attained and income received. It is our "common sense" that tells us that achieved education has some value in explaining income, but not vice versa. Our common sense tells us this because we know that income is being received in the present; achieved education typically occurred in the past. You cannot explain something by citing as its cause something that took place later in time. Common sense also suggests that, given a relationship between an unalterable phenomenon such as age (race, sex) and some other characteristic, such as income or education, the former must be influencing the latter but not vice versa.

Another notion about theories discussed in the last chapter and shown to be false stated that "The word 'theory' means the same thing as the word 'prediction.'" At this point a distinction needs to be made between two terms whose meanings are often combined under the one term "prediction": extrapolation and prediction. *Extrapolation refers to taking a trend which can be documented to exist and "predicting" the future as a simple continuation of that trend.* The basis for extrapolation is research into the recent past; by itself it involves no theory or explanation and, for that very reason, is very often wrong. For instance one might graph the birth rates of a nation over the past decade or even the past century. If a trend line appears in the past, extrapolation involves simply extending that line into the future, as depicted in Chart

18

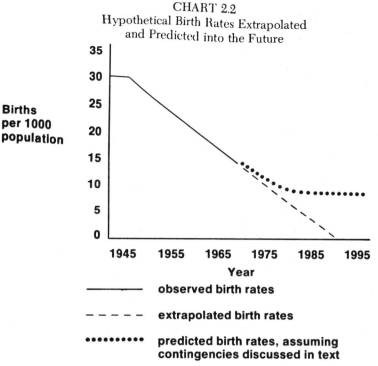

CHART 2.2
Hypothetical Birth Rates Extrapolated
and Predicted into the Future

Births per 1000 population

— observed birth rates

– – – – – extrapolated birth rates

•••••••••• predicted birth rates, assuming
contingencies discussed in text

2.2. The rate at which something occurs is assumed, in this approach, not to change. The potential ridiculousness of the procedure is seen in this chart. Extrapolating from a given rate of decline in the birth rate, by about 1990 this hypothetical nation would be "expected" to have no births at all! Many estimates of future population figures have been made without too much more sophistication than this, and quite often they have been very wrong. When amateurs dabble in the stock market they are often engaged in extrapolative thinking and often learn the painful way how unreliable this approach is! However, in the absence of other information extrapolation may provide some useful insights, at least in terms of the short run or near future.

Prediction, as separate from extrapolation, is based on an understanding of why observed trends are as they are; it is a guess about the future rooted in a comprehension of the reasons behind past occurrences. When predictions are wrong, we know that there is something the matter with the theories upon which they were based. Thus, for instance, if some of the reasons behind high and low birth rates are

19

understood, instead of assuming that a present trend will automatically continue (extrapolation), a prediction might be made which states certain contingencies: the gradually declining birth rate experienced over the past decade will not reverse itself if women continue to experience rising employment rates and greater economic opportunities; it will gradually cease to fall further and level off at a low rate (see Chart 2.2). This prediction is rooted in an explanation of birth rates which claims that, in a society capable of controlling reproduction, women will choose to have fewer children (not zero!) if roles other than motherhood (especially work roles) are readily available and, conversely, will elect to have more children when work roles are less available. Why do women have several children? Because they have few other viable roles to play to consume their time and attention. We have here a minitheory, an explanation, upon which a prediction can be based. If economic opportunities for women were to continue to expand but the birth rate rose, our explanation would have to be considered wrong. If our prediction comes true, then we have support for (but never final proof of) our explanation. Note, however, that the prediction emanates from the explanation; it is not the explanation per se.

In the example just cited the prediction concerning birth rates hinges on a contingency: rising employment rates and greater economic opportunities for women. A large array of factors can influence whether or not and to what extent this contingency is realized. A severe economic recession, a change in governmental and/or judicial policy, or cultural changes in the definitions of women's roles, for instance, could all impact the extent of economic opportunity available to women. Thus, we are predicting that, *given certain conditions*, birth rates will remain low.

B. CONJUNCTURE, CONTINGENCY, AND CONTROLLED EXPERIMENTS

Prediction in the social sciences is overwhelmingly of the type described in the preceding example, that is, based on contingencies over which control may not be exercisable. This may be contrasted with the laboratory setting, in which physical scientists can often control or account for all of the factors which presumably impact the phenomenon in question. To the extent that their explanation of why something changes (or takes on different values) is correct, they are able to predict that, in a given experiment, a particular type of change will definitely occur. For instance, in a laboratory setting a chemist is able to predict with great accuracy the density of gas molecules because the two variables which determine density, temperature and pressure, can be precisely controlled.

Physical scientists are not always able to control the factors which influence the phenomenon in question. Meteorologists cannot, for instance, control wind patterns and velocities or temperature changes. When physical scientists are unable to exert such control they are in the same situation in which social scientists typically find themselves. Even if those who study human behavior were able to control all the myriad influences, past and present, that presumably collectively result in a given behavior or event under examination, ethical considerations would prohibit such control. Some sociologists and social psychologists do conduct laboratory experiments. However, even in the laboratory setting total control is impossible for social scientists. Unlike gases and atoms, human behavior reflects, however dimly, constantly changing interpretations and perceptions, as well as all the experiences which have constituted the total life of the person. These are scarcely amenable to strict laboratory control!

The result of this lack of control is that predictions in the social sciences are stochastic. *"Stochastic" is a synonym for probabilistic.* Just as weather is forecast in terms of "a 60 percent chance of rain today," sociologists might predict that "there is a 70 percent chance of a race riot occurring during the next decade." The occurrence of a specific event in time and space cannot be predicted because it is the result of the accidental coming together of the various contingencies, or conjuncture. *Conjuncture is defined as the "interaction between phenomena in concrete time and space"* (Timasheff, 1959, p. 162). The point here is that a given event may be explained as the result of a series of causal chains which accidentally meet in a particular place at a specific time. The event in question can be explained *after* it has occurred but cannot be predicted because of the accidental nature of when and where the causal chains come together. For instance, suppose a pedestrian is crossing a street and is struck by a car. The pedestrian was in a hurry because she was late for an important meeting and, therefore, failed to notice the signal to wait. The car was running an amber light because its driver was engrossed in thoughts of a meeting to which he too was headed. We have an explanation for why each party to the accident was in that particular place at that time and why each was careless in

21

negotiating the intersection. We can, therefore, "explain" the occurrence of that pedestrian-car collision. However, it was a matter of pure historical accident that that particular careless pedestrian intersected in physical space with that particular careless driver, an accident requiring split-second timing. All that we are able to say before the fact is that, given a substantial number of careless pedestrians and drivers, there is a high probability that sooner or later some of them will collide. This is the nature of much sociological prediction and explanation.

C. Types of Explanations

There are a number of different ways to answer the question "why?" Only a few are important to sociologists. Many scientists consider that the best way to answer this question is to provide a list of conditions which together are considered necessary and sufficient to explain the occurrence of the phenomenon in question. *A necessary explanation is one in which the elements listed must be present to bring about the result in question.* Clouds are necessary to bring about rain; it is impossible to have rainfall in the total absence of clouds. However, it does not rain every time there are clouds. Therefore, clouds are not sufficient to create rain. *A sufficient explanation is one in which the elements listed will always bring about the result in question.* The presence of a fair quantity of strychnine in the body will always bring about sickness and, if untreated, death. In large enough dosage, strychnine is, therefore, a sufficient cause of death. However, there are a lot of other substances beside strychnine which can result in sickness and death, so that strychnine is not necessary to cause them. An increase in the temperature surrounding a normally functioning mercury thermometer is both necessary and sufficient to cause a rise in the mercury column. That column will not rise for any other reason (if the thermometer is functioning properly) and will always rise when the temperature is elevated.

Despite claims to the contrary, in sociology there are, to my knowledge, no explanations which constitute complete statements of necessary and sufficient causes. Indeed, there are few explanations that constitute full statements of the necessary *or* sufficient causes of an event or behavior. An example of the former is Lenski's argument (1966) that, for a system of social stratification to develop, it is necessary that the collectivity produce an economic surplus, that is, more than the minimum required to sustain the lives of the individuals within the collectivity. Since it is possible to distribute any surplus equally, the existence of such a surplus is probably not sufficient to explain the rise of systems of social stratification or inequality. A rather loose statement concerning rates of intergenerational upward social mobility exemplifies sufficient explanations in sociology. Bendix and Lipset (1964) argue that a certain level (unspecified but presumably fairly high) of industrialization creates a relatively high (but also unspecified) rate of intergenerational upward social mobility in societies. Industrialization appears to be a sufficient explanation for high rates of upward mobility because of the related changes in employment structure which result. The relative proportion of white-collar jobs increases while that of blue-collar jobs decreases, thus "forcing" intergenerational upward mobility. However, it is unlikely that this constitutes a necessary explanation, since for instance, political policies based on egalitarian ideologies could possibly produce the same results.

A very important type of explanation for social scientists is functional explanation. A word of caution: do not confuse functional explanation as a general type with the particular use of this approach employed by some sociologists called "Structural-Functionalists" (e.g., Talcott Parsons) and sometimes shortened to just "Functionalists."

In order to understand the meaning of the term "functional explanation" it is necessary first to understand the general concepts "system," "feedback," and "equilibrium." *A system is any series of elements characterized by the fact that they interact in such a manner that when change occurs in any one element, the other elements tend to change in response.* For example, in the normally functioning human body, if muscular activity increases in the arms and legs (for instance, through exercise), the heart will respond by pumping harder and the lungs will work harder taking in air and expelling waste. The functioning of the muscles, heart, and lungs in this case constitute the system in question. Clearly, there are many other elements in the body system which could also have been included. The scientist must draw the line, so to speak, and specify which elements are of interest at a given time for purposes of a given explanation.

If the scientist includes in the theory all the elements which comprise the system, then we talk of *closed systems;* everything needed to explain change in any of the constituent parts is included. If, as most typically occurs in sociology, the scientist is unable to specify all elements that comprise the system, then we speak of *open systems*. In this case there is specific recognition that other elements can and do influence those which constitute the system, but they are unknown and/or too numerous to specify in the theory. An example of an open systems concept which has been used (and hotly debated) in sociology concerns poverty. Some observers speak of a culture of poverty, namely, a set of values and attitudes which are short-range and fatalistic, which is related to unemployment, lack of education and skill, high rates of illegitimate births, high rates of family desertion by husband-fathers, criminal activity, alcohol and drug abuse, and other problems. These various traits (as well as others which are not specified) are, presumably, all interrelated so that each is constantly affecting the others within poor families and communities.

In all systems there is an additional feature beyond the direct interaction of the elements defined as constituting the system, namely, feedback. *Feedback refers to the fact that not only does change in one element give rise to change in the other elements, but, in turn, the original element is further changed in response to the changes in the other elements.* For instance, let us assume that the elements listed above do interact systemically and let us further assume that a recession causes an increase in unemployment in an already poor group. This increase should bring about an increase in the fatalism and short-range orientation known as the culture of poverty, as well as in criminality, alcohol and drug abuse, family desertion, and so on. Each of these, in turn, should impact the employability of group members, further exacerbating the unemployment rates of the group. This is an example of feedback.

Many but not all systems share another characteristic known as *equilibrium* or *homeostasis*. This concept refers to a *tendency toward self-correction; for alterations in system elements to be met by counterchanges.* The household heating and cooling mechanism is an equilibrating system. The equilibrium point is the temperature at which the thermostat is set. The temperature will rise to a point somewhat above that temperature and then an automatic response is triggered (in this case an air-conditioning or heating unit will go on or off) to lower it. When lowered somewhat beyond the point of equilibrium an automatic response will occur (the machine will go off or on) in order to raise the temperature, and so on endlessly. The healthy human body is also a homeostatic system. When a foreign virus or bacteria invades it, certain body processes automatically go to work in an attempt to return the system to its previous functioning (by the production of more white blood cells).

Many theorists argue (and others strongly disagree) that social systems are also self-controlling, that is, they constitute systems tending toward equilibrium. To argue in this fashion necessitates the ability to specify the nature of the equilibrating mechansim, much as scientists are able to specify what the human body does to fight invasion by a foreign body or technicians can explain how the thermostat works. Sociologists, however, find it more difficult to explain what societies do to resist change. Such explanation also necessitates the ability to specify with some precision what "normal functioning" or the equilibrium point is. We know within some fairly narrow range of individual differences what a "healthy body" is; do we know what a "healthy society" is? Sociological theories that contain a concept of equilibrium (such as Parsons' Structural-Functional theory [1951]) basically assume that social change occurs only very slowly and gradually due to this inherent homeostatic tendency of the system. More rapid and extensive efforts toward change would tend to be met by strong reactions in the opposite direction. Many sociologists have rejected equilibrium theories because of this approach to social change, which, they argue, ignores more rapid and dramatic instances of change. Other bases of rejection include the two mentioned above (what is a "healthy society?" and what precisely is the nature of the equilibrating mechanism in societies?), and the assertion that such theories engage in reification, a problem to be discussed in Chapter 4.

Functional explanations, whether or not a concept of equilibrium is built in, *answer the question "why?" by pointing to the system of which the variable in question is a part.* Why is there high unemployment in a particular poverty community? Because unemployment is one element in a system of specified elements which, *collectively,* explains the element in question. This approach differs from necessary and sufficient explanation in a crucial way. In the later case a temporal dimension is always assumed. Something cannot be a necessary and/or sufficient cause of something else unless it happens prior to that which you are explaining. In functional explanation no time sequence is assumed. Often, various elements change simultaneously or, when they change sequentially, any one can precede any other and, in fact, succeed it as well. In short, in functional explanations, changes continually

25

reverberate throughout the system, back and forth (via feedback) in no predetermined sequence or order.

D. Some Common Problems in Explanation

Certain problems which must be consciously avoided frequently arise in creating explanations. Two are especially important. The first is the problem of *tautology*. A tautology is a *statement that is true by definition; it cannot be falsified*. It may also be seen as "circular reasoning." There is nothing wrong with definitions unless they are treated as explanations, at which point they become tautologies. Suppose, for instance, that we say that the term "deviance" means the breaking of social norms and that John and Mary are deviants. "Why are they deviants?" someone asks. "Because they failed to conform to the rule that says that it's the woman who stays home with the children and the man who goes to work." This is not an explanation, even though it may sound like one. It is an example of a type of social deviance, defined as rule breaking. We still do not know why John and Mary have broken this social convention. If this statement is taken as an explanation, then we have an example of tautology. Another example might be:

"Fran is smart."

"Why is Fran smart?"

"Because she has a high IQ."

One way of defining "smart" or intelligent is achieving a high score on the IQ test. Therefore, a high IQ doesn't explain Fran's smartness; it is part of the definition of her smartness.

A second, common problem in designing explanations involves *teleology*. A teleology *occurs when the explanation cites the result of something as its cause*. Teleologies may be very subtle and difficult to perceive. People often engage in activities precisely in order to bring about desired goals. When they do that, it is appropriate to say that the result (or, more accurately, the anticipation of the result) caused the behavior. Why did John go to college? In order to get a better job after graduation. The better job, the future result, was anticipated and could thus legitimately be said to explain the prior activity of attending college. Often, however, this same logic is used when analyzing units that are incapable of anticipation and when that happens we have a teleology. Why do communities develop a division of labor after they reach a certain population size? In order to reduce competition between

26

people over scarce resources. A reduction in resource competition may indeed result from division of labor, as Durkheim argued (1947). It is highly unlikely, however, that a community of people sat down and said to itself, "Let's see. If we divide up all the work so that each of us specializes, we won't come into direct competition with one another." In this case, an anticipated result cannot have provided the cause of the phenomenon in question (the division of labor) because the unit (the prespecialized community) did not anticipate the result. The explanation is teleological.

The discussion of teleology highlights the necessity of distinguishing the causes which explain the occurrence of a given phenomenon and the results or consequences (sometimes also called "functions") of the occurrence of that same phenomenon. They are both important to examine, but such examination will not progress if they are confused with one another. In theory construction and testing attention is generally focused on delineating causes. In applying our scientific understandings to the real world, it is important to pay attention to and try to anticipate consequences.

The sociologist Robert K. Merton pointed to a distinction in types of consequences, which he called "functions" (1957, pp. 19-84). Understanding this distinction can spell the difference between disastrous and successful application of social scientific knowledge to real world problems. He spoke of *manifest and latent consequences* (functions). *Manifest consequences are the anticipated or planned results of an action. Latent consequences are the unanticipated, often long-range results.* Although sometimes the latent consequences may provide an unexpected bonus, all too often in public policy they have either obliterated the positive benefits accruing from the manifest consequences, created a host of new problems, or even served in the long-run to make the original problem worse. For instance, after World War II, in an attempt to raise the quality of life for Americans, the federal government spent tremendous sums of money to develop suburbs. It did this primarily through low-interest home mortgages to veterans and through highway development linking the suburbs to central cities. Millions of people did indeed experience a marked improvement in the quality of life as they moved to newer, more spacious, less crowded homes and communities. Some of the long-term, latent consequences of these policies have, however, proven disastrous for cities, other groups of people, and indeed the migrants themselves. To name a few of these

27

latent consequences: the central cities lost a good share of their tax base as middle- and working-class people left for the suburbs, eventually to be followed by many of their employers who moved factories and offices out along the highways. Central cities are thus increasingly left to the poor and without the tax base to provide needed services. Areawide air pollution, the result largely of auto emissions, is another latent consequence of policies which encouraged people to move out of central cities and daily drive back in. Finally, the improved quality of life that was to result from living in the suburbs has often proven to be a life of isolation and boredom for many housewives and teenagers who yearn for the excitement, proximity to services, and personal contacts of urban living.

The message to be learned is that the more long-term "side effects" we can anticipate to result from a given policy, the better will be our policy formation. However, by their very nature we can never anticipate all the latent consequences of our actions. Therefore, we must expect and tolerate the fact that new problems will always be emerging that require imaginative solutions, which will, themselves, often if not usually help to create further problems.

E. EXEMPLAR

In the final section of the last chapter, the basic issues about which two colleagues and I are attempting to theorize were presented. Recall that we are trying to explain two phenomena: (1) differential rates of employment over time among women and racial/ethnic minorities compared to white males; (2) differential occupational deployment (what groups hold what kinds of jobs) when contrasting the same groups over time. Stated more fully, we wish first to explain the conditions under which social minority group members are employed at rates that are similar to (and different from) those of the social majority (white males). Second, under what conditions do the types of jobs performed by women and minority group members resemble (or sharply differ from) those performed by white males?

The theory is presented schematically in Chart 2.3 (taken from Chafetz, Dworkin and Dworkin, 1976). No attempt will be made to explain the entire model at this stage of the book. The reader will need to refer back to this chart in subsequent chapters. Several features will be pointed out now that exemplify issues raised in this chapter.

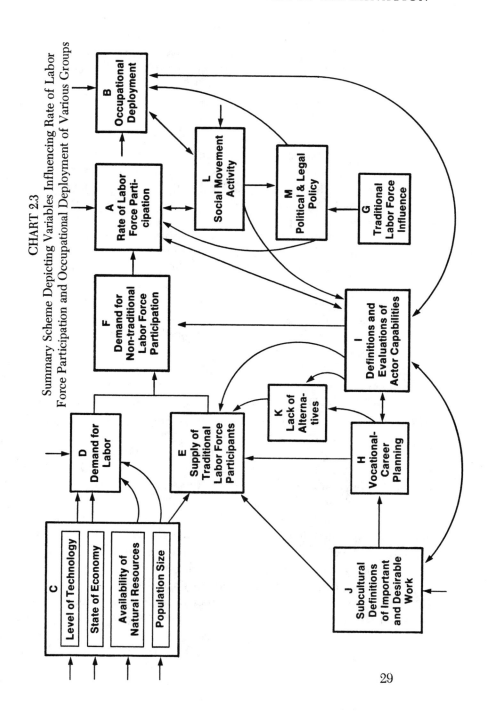

CHART 2.3
Summary Scheme Depicting Variables Influencing Rate of Labor
Force Participation and Occupational Deployment of Various Groups

The two variables which we are trying to explain are located in the upper right hand corner and lettered A and B. Arrows pointed into any given box in the diagram denote direct causal influence of one element upon another. Arrows which do not originate in a box denote our recognition that other, unspecified variables also influence the one in question. This feature shows that our theory is an *open* rather than closed one.

Despite some recent evidence that women and some minority groups are increasingly similar to white males in the relevant ways, this model does not predict a continued rise in labor force participation for women and/or minorities; nor does it predict that their occupational deployment patterns will be increasingly similar to that of white males. Nor, in fact, does it predict the opposite. It attempts to *predict* (not extrapolate) the conditions under which women and minority groups will tend to be more or less similar to white males in both dimensions. Thus, the model is *contingency-based* and *stochastic*. At the far left are four boxes, collectively labeled C, which include elements which indirectly have enormous impact on A and B. These elements cannot be controlled nor can their values be precisely predicted into the future. Thus, the contingent nature of this model is underscored. It is the *conjunction* of the four elements which comprise C that impacts a key variable, labeled in Chart 2.3 as D. What this tells us is that when a series of uncontrollable conditions (C) interact at a specific time to increase (or decrease) the demand for labor (D), then, depending on a series of other conditions which impact the supply of labor which usually does the work in question (labeled E), the demand for other kinds of people (F), will rise (or fall). It is F, or the demand for people who have not heretofore worked, that directly impacts A and indirectly impacts B. A more detailed discussion of the meanings of these elements and the ways in which they interact will be undertaken in Chapters 4 and 6.

The variables that comprise this theory are not all directly related to each other, although there are indirect linkages between most. Thus, this model could be viewed as a more or less *open-systems type of functional explanation*. However, since we are not attempting to explain changes fully in many of the other variables and since the important elements listed as C are not impacted by the other variables in the model, it may be better viewed as an attempt to provide a *necessary but not sufficient explanation* of A and B.

There are two additional features to note. First, there is *no notion of equilibrium* built in; indeed it is a model of change. Forces are identified which will tend to resist change (e.g., traditional labor force influence, or G). However, there is no direct implication that those forces will usually tend to prevent substantial change from occurring. Whether or not change occurs is primarily a function of C, which is not directly impacted by any of the other variables in the theory.

Second, many of the variables are involved in *feedback* loops, as indicated most directly by the double pointed arrows. If you trace the various arrows carefully you will find several examples of indirect feedback as well. Let us examine one simple example each of direct and indirect feedback. The degree to which members of a group (women, blacks, Chicanos, etc.) develop employment-related skills is represented in box H. This results in part from the way in which group members and others in the society define their capabilities (I). If, for instance, women are defined and/or define themselves as having "no head for numbers" they will not acquire the mathematical training necessary to become engineers and other technical and scientific types of personnel. In turn, as represented by the double pointed arrow, the skills possessed by group members affects their own and others' definitions of their capabilities. When a large number of women fail to learn mathematical skills, the stereotypes which say they can't are reinforced. An example of indirect feedback is provided by examining the boxes labeled H, I, and J. The definitions of actor capabilities of a group (I) affect the extent to which group members define a given type of job as important and desirable (J). If, for instance, Japanese-Americans are defined (as they long were) as good gardeners, they will be more apt to define agriculture, horticulture, and the biological sciences as important and desirable spheres of activity. This, in turn, provides the motivation for Japanese-Americans to seek training in these areas (H) which, as we saw above, further impacts definitions of the capabilities of group members (I).

To sum up, we think we have developed a theory with the following characteristics: it provides a necessary but not sufficient explanation of the two phenomena in question; it is an open-ended, contingency-based, stochastic theory with several feedback mechanisms. This theory avoids tautology by independently defining the various elements, which will be demonstrated in Chapter 4. It also avoids teleology inasmuch as we are not imputing purposeful action except where people are involved who can act on the basis of anticipated future consequences (e.g., boxes G, H,

J, and others to be discussed later). Nor are we claiming that changes in either direction in A and B will necessarily occur because of some consequential end state.

STUDENT EXERCISES

1. State each of the following as a regular English sentence and then attempt to develop an explanation based on the correlation given (you may need to add more variables). For each try to think of yet other variables that might make the relationship spurious.
   a. -.300 correlation between age and time spent listening to the radio.
   b. +.455 correlation between number of friends people have and their income.
   c. +.675 correlation between the number of terms a person has served in Congress and the amount of contributions to her/his last campaign.
2. For each of the following develop an explanation; then state the type of explanation it is (necessary, sufficient, both, functional). Why do you say it is that type?
   a. Your grade point average last term (treat it as good, bad, or fair).
   b. The reason you are doing this exercise.
   c. Why students choose the majors they do.
3. What is wrong with each of the following explanations? Rewrite each in some fashion so that there is no longer an error.
   a. Why are we poor? Because we don't earn enough money.
   b. The reason Joe was elected president of the club is that he is the most popular.
   c. Poverty persists because so many middle-class people make their living serving the needs of the poor.
3. Select a governmental (national, state, or local) policy with which you are familiar. Specify its manifest consequences. What are (or if it has only been in effect a short time, what might be) some of its latent consequences? Do the same for a policy formulated by one of your professors for a course you are taking.

CHAPTER 3

Assumptions: The Underpinnings of Theories

In everyday life assumptions are those things that are taken for granted about the world—out of faith, ignorance, factual knowledge, or previous experience. You assume that, despite the fact that it has rained for two weeks, sooner or later there will be a sunny day because "that's the way the world has always been." Some people assume that the only reason people ever work hard is to make more money because "greed is a component of human nature," while others assume that, under the right conditions people work hard in order to express an innate need for creativity. We all make hundreds of assumptions about our world in everyday life, usually without thinking about them.

Assumptions are also part of the world of science. *Scientific assumptions are statements taken as given and not subject to direct empirical verification (testing).* They are generally made in two cases: when something is intrinsically not amenable to empirical proof or disproof (e.g., the nature of reality), and when the present state of knowledge does not allow us to prove or disprove something (e.g., whether or not humans are innately aggressive). Often, however, we are unable to say whether we don't know because it is impossible to know or because we don't yet have the tools that will enable us to know.

Scientists, like everyone else, make a variety of assumptions about the world they study. Often they are unaware of the many assumptions which underpin their theories. It is, however, extremely important for theorists to be as self-conscious and explicit about their assumptions as humanly possible. Where they fail to make their own assumptions clear, it is important for readers to attempt to ferret out of their works the implicit assumptions.

A properly constructed theory is a logical system which begins with a series of "givens," which are not going to be further questioned. In any system of logic, once the initial "givens" or premises have been accepted, the conclusions derived from them by the proper use of logic must also be accepted. To reject logically derived conclusions after accepting the premises upon which they are based constitutes an exercise in emotionally based prejudice. When tempted to reject such conclusions, you will typically find upon examination that you in fact reject one or more of the original premises. In a given theory there may be premises based in factual knowledge (e.g., women have a longer life expectancy than men); there may also be premises which are assumptions (e.g., women are the weaker sex). In the latter case it is important to decide first on whether or not to accept a theorist's assumptions because once you do, you will often be "hooked" into the entire argument which follows.

A. GENERAL SCIENTIFIC ASSUMPTIONS

The scientific process, irrespective of the particular science, requires certain very general assumptions about reality and how we come to know reality. These assumptions are often broadly accepted in the non-scientific community as well, but they need not be.

As simple as it may seem, all scientists must assume that there is a reality that exists "out there"; life is not an illusion that exists only in the subjective minds of people. Not only must science assume the existence of reality outside individual human minds, but it must also assume that human beings are capable of knowing or comprehending that reality, of discerning with substantial accuracy the nature of that reality. Another way of saying this is to point out that all sciences seek to understand some aspect of empirical reality. Scientists must thus assume that they are potentially capable of knowing that reality "out there." Moreover, all sciences assume that it is through the direct and indirect use of our senses that we can know that reality. Divine revelation, pure subjective

34

introspection, and other methods of knowing are not acceptable means of acquiring scientific knowledge. This is not to say, however, that such methods are unacceptable means of acquiring any knowledge. After all, science does not provide the only mode of knowing; it is one way among many. But, to the extent that we wish to acquire scientific knowledge about something, we must assume that the phenomena involved may and must be observed and measured, however crudely or imperfectly, through the direct or indirect application of one or more of our senses (hearing, seeing, tasting, smelling, feeling).

The scientific process requires the further assumption that there is order in the universe and that this order is also comprehensible by human beings. If each event, process, and phenomenon were absolutely unique and/or occurred randomly (i.e., without order or pattern), there could be no generalization. Without generalization there is no science. In other words, all sciences attempt to generalize about recurrent phenomena. This attempt presupposes an orderly, nonrandom world. Imagine, for instance, how far we could get in an attempt to understand crime if each and every incident of criminal activity were totally unique in why and how it was committed, what types of people committed it, how it was treated by others, and so on.

The assumption of an orderly universe is closely connected to another important assumption made by all sciences. Unlike at least some philosophers and theologians, scientists must assume causality, or the logical connection between perceivable events, processes, and other phenomena, through which an action by one element brings about (i.e., causes) an action by another or other elements. Thus, for instance, in science there can be no such thing as "free will," in so far as free will implies that behavior could be caused by nothing more than a metaphysical attribute that cannot be perceived directly or indirectly by any of the senses. In short, the concept of free will denies causality in human behavior and in so doing results in a view of human behavior that contradicts the assumption of an orderly, nonrandom universe. This is not to deny that humans have choices and alternatives in most everything they do. It is to say that the social and behavioral sciences assume that the alternatives are limited and patterned and that the choices made are orderly (nonrandom) and caused by other (at least potentially knowable) phenomena concerning the person and/or situation. Thus, the assumption is made that human behavior is neither predetermined in the strict, extreme sense of the word nor the product

35

of "free will." In a less strict or extreme usage, however, humans, like all phenomena in the universe, behave in a deterministic fashion; that is, what occurs is at least potentially amenable to causal explanation which cites the factors which predispose the activity or action in question.

All these assumptions which underpin the exercise of science are also part and parcel of the everyday lives of all people. We might hold religious and/or philosophical beliefs which contradict some of these assumptions. However, we usually behave as if we accepted them. For instance, we assume that there is a reality "out there" and that we can know it through our senses every time we take action to avoid walking into a wall or a piece of furniture. We assume an orderly universe and causality every time we attempt to explain something to ourselves or someone else without reference to a deity or other unverifiable being or attribute. In short, when we are not acting on the basis of pure faith, we are usually acting on the basis of the general assumptions enumerated in this section.

B. Paradigms

At any given time, each science consists of one or more general ways of approaching the subject matter of the particular discipline. These general orientations are based on assumptions concerning the nature of the reality in question, the questions that are important to ask of that reality, and the best way to attempt to answer those questions. In his seminal work, *The Structure of Scientific Revolutions,* first published in 1962, Thomas Kuhn called these general orientations *"paradigms,"* and that term has been widely adopted by sociologists. A more complete discussion of the meaning of the word "paradigm" is offered by Ritzer (1975, p. 7):

> A paradigm is a fundamental image of the subject matter within a science. It serves to define what should be studied, what questions should be asked, how they should be asked, and what rules should be followed in interpreting the answers obtained. The paradigm is the broadest unit of consensus within a science and serves to differentiate one scientific community (or *sub-community*) from another. It subsumes, defines, and inter-relates the examples, theories, and methods and instruments that exist within it.

If a given science has one widely agreed upon paradigm, its efforts are spent doing those things we usually think of as the "normal" scientific process: developing theories, testing them, revising them, retesting, and so on. Every so often a *"scientific revolution"* occurs, such as that created by Einstein with the introduction into physics of the concept of relativity. A scientific revolution marks the rather dramatic point at which a new paradigm gains sufficient acceptance within a science to replace an old one (in this case Newtonian mechanics). The new paradigm is able to replace the theories of the old and go beyond these to explain facts that are anomalies, that is, inexplicable, under the old approach. It is established on the basis of a different set of assumptions concerning the issues delineated in the quote from Ritzer. After the new paradigm gains consensus within the science, a period of "normal science" follows until enough anomalies accumulate to result in a new scientific revolution. The process is never ending.

Many sciences are not characterized by one ascendent paradigm which enjoys broad consensus; they are multiple-paradigm sciences. According to Ritzer (1975, p. 12):

> One of the defining characteristics of a multiple-paradigm science is that supporters of one paradigm are constantly questioning the basic assumptions of those who accept other paradigms. Thus, scientists have a difficult time conducting "normal science" because they are constantly defending their flanks against attacks from those who support other paradigms.

Sociology is a multiparadigm science (as all social and behavioral sciences tend to be) and thus prey to constant debate concerning basic assumptions. While almost all sociologists would agree that there is no one dominant paradigm in the field today, there is no consensus on how many paradigms currently exist.

At a very minimum there are two widely differing sociological paradigms with large numbers of followers in the contemporary United States. Ritzer calls these the "social factist" and "social definitionist" paradigms. (He also identifies a third, the "social behaviorist," which is more debatable as a widely accepted sociological paradigm.) The social factist paradigm can be dated back to Durkheim and has among its modern adherents both Conflict and Consensus theorists. (Other scholars claim Conflict and Consensus approaches are themselves two separate paradigms.) The social definitionist paradigm can be dated back to Weber and has among its modern adherents Labeling theorists,

Symbolic Interactionists, Phenomenologists, and Ethnomethodologists. Let us examine these two paradigms somewhat more closely.

The social factist paradigm generally assumes that what sociology ought to study are phenomena that are external to individuals and have a coercive influence on the actions of individuals. Social facts include norms, roles, customs, rites, rates of various behaviors, and so forth. They are assumed to have a reality that is independent of any individual and can thus be studied in essentially the same fashion as material objects. Within this paradigm, the sociologist is supposed to relate social facts to one another, explaining the existence of any one with reference only to others, thereby avoiding psychological, biological, or other types of *"reductionism,"* that is, *explanations of social facts by reference to nonsocial phenomena.* Stated another way, human collectivities and the sociocultural products of collectivities are assumed to have a reality that is separate and distinct from individuals. They are capable of being studied independently and comprise the subject matter of sociology.

One example of this type of study is Durkheim's *Suicide* (1897). In this work Durkheim developed a theory to explain why different categories of people (e.g., the married vs the unmarried, Catholics compared to Jews and Protestants, etc.) have different suicide rates. He did not ask why a given individual might kill him or herself (a psychological question); he asked why groups of people differ in the rate at which their members kill themselves (a question about a social fact: suicide rates). In response to the first question one might answer such things as "he lost his love" or "she was ruined financially." In contrast Durkheim's answers involved two types of culturally based reasons, known as altruistic suicide and anomic suicide, and a social-structural reason known as egoistic suicide. In altruistic suicide a group experiences a high rate of suicide because custom dictates the taking of one's life under certain circumstances (e.g., Hindu widow suicide called *suttee* and the Japanese Kamikaze pilots of World War II). In anomic suicide a group experiences high rates because of the absence of norms which define legitimate aspirations for group members who are thus perpetually dissatisfied with life. In egoistic suicide, high rates occur among groups which lack the means of integrating people into cohesive social units or communities. In short, the question asked, the data gathered, and the answers provided all concern social rather than individual facts.

The social definitionist paradigm generally assumes that what sociology ought to study are human actions to which the individual actors attach subjective meaning and in which the individual takes into account the actions of other humans (whether or not they are present). The emphasis in this paradigm falls on the subjective states of interacting individuals, who are often viewed as creating their own social reality. This view is captured succinctly by the famous dictum of W.I. Thomas (1923) that if one defines a situation as real (regardless of the accuracy of that definition), it is real in its social consequences. The questions raised thus tend to be those pertaining to how people perceive and interpret others and themselves in a social context. One means by which it is assumed that such questions may be answered was called by Weber *verstehen*. The term *"verstehen"* (which is not usually translated but rather is used in the original German) *can be translated as "interpretive understanding" or, sometimes, "empathic understanding."* It refers to an effort to understand human behavior in terms of actors' motives; of trying to assume mentally the "shoes" of others, and, through introspection, figure out how they define the situation.

The two paradigms discussed are similar to although not identical with the often used distinction between social-structural and social-psychological approaches to sociological theory. It should be clear that the social factist and social definitionist approaches differ in every way listed by Ritzer as relevant to defining a paradigm. Their most fundamental difference is that they begin with substantially different assumptions about the nature of social reality. From this basic difference flow the other differences noted.

C. Domain Assumptions

Assumptions which are relatively specific to the subject matter of a theory have been called by Alvin Gouldner "domain assumptions." Such assumptions are pervasive in sociological theory, but quite often they are not explicitly stated. According to Gouldner, they arise and operate in much the same manner as social stereotypes and prejudices (1970, p. 33):

(1) There is a disposition to believe that there are certain attributes that will be manifested by *all* members of the domain, which (2) is acquired well before the believer has had a personal experience with anything like a true sample of the members of the domain . . . but which (3) may, nonetheless, entail the strongest feelings about them, (4) shape his [or her]

39

subsequent encounters with them, and that (5) are not at all easily shaken or changed, even when these encounters produce experiences discrepant with the assumptions.

The number of domain assumptions made by at least some sociologists is enormous. They differ substantially in how broad a scope (or large a domain) they cover. Some are relatively narrow, referring to a group (e.g., racial or sexual category), a culture, or a society. Others are broad, referring to "human nature" or societies in general. Some very broad domain assumptions which have been made by at least a few major social thinkers include: humans are fundamentally irrational (or rational); societies are fundamentally stable (or constantly changing); humans enter the world with a *tabula rasa* so that what they become is purely a matter of sociocultural conditioning; humans are innately propelled to express themselves through creative work; humans need to be constrained by group or governmental controls in order to live with any degree of satisfaction (or group and governmental constraint are the root of all human misery); and so on in an almost endless list.

Domain assumptions are important to understand because they often reflect underlying sociopolitical values and orientations. Theories may thus be subtly infused with political content quite apart from their scientific meaning. This can be seen when the long-standing, often acrimonious debate between Conflict and Consensus theorists is examined. Terming the former "radicals" and the latter "conservatives," Lenski identified several basic assumptions upon which they differ (1966, pp. 22-23):

1. . . . conservatives have been distrustful of man's [sic] basic nature and have emphasized the need for restraining social institutions . . . radicals have been distrustful of these restraining institutions and have taken an optimistic view of man's [sic] nature.
2. . . . conservatives have traditionally viewed society as a social system with various needs of its own which must be met if the needs and desires of its constituent members are to be met. Radicals . . . have tended to view society more as the setting within which various struggles take place. . . .
3. Radicals have generally emphasized coercion as the chief factor undergirding and maintaining private property . . . and other institutions which give rise to unequal rights and privileges. Conservatives . . . have argued that coercion plays only a minor role and inequality arises as a necessary consequence of consensus . . . and/or innate differences. . . .

4. . . . proponents of the two traditions have differed concerning the degree to which inequality in society generates conflict. Radicals have seen this as one of the chief consequences of inequality; conservatives have generally minimized it.

5. Radicals have laid great emphasis on force, fraud, and inheritance as the chief avenues [by which rights and privileges are acquired]. Conservatives . . . have stressed more justifiable methods such as hard work, delegation by others, and so forth.

6. . . . conservatives have always regarded inequality as inevitable. Radicals . . . have taken the opposite view. . . .

7. . . . a major disagreement has always existed with respect to the nature of the state and of law. Radicals have . . . regarded both as instruments of oppression employed by the ruling classes for their own benefit. Conservatives have seen them as organs of the total society, acting basically to promote the common good.

Since scientists are human beings not basically different from other people, it must be remembered, as Gouldner took pains to point out, that their domain assumptions can be just as "irrational" as the prejudices of others. By the very nature of assumptions, they are not rooted in verified, scientific knowledge. They often reflect the culture and sub-culture in which the scientist lives, his or her family background, religion, and so forth. This is especially the case among those who study nonbiological aspects of human beings, namely, social and behavioral scientists, including, of course, sociologists. Given this tendency for personal and political values and cultural ethnocentrism to influence the domain assumptions underpinning social theories, it is especially important for a reader to play detective when the theorist is less than highly explicit (the usual case) in stating her or his assumptions. One aid to this process is some knowledge about the historical era, culture, and intellectual and personal history of the theorist(s) in question.

D. Exemplar

As in any scientific enterprise, the theory my colleagues and I are developing assumes all the things discussed in Section A of this chapter under the heading "General Scientific Assumptions." We are attempting to develop a scientific, not philosophical or theological, explanation of the phenomena in question.

The elements of our theory do not all fall precisely within one or the other of the two basic sociological paradigms. However, there is a far

41

greater emphasis on a "social factist" approach than on a "social definitionist" one. The two elements we are attempting to explain, comparative rates of labor force participation and patterns of occupational deployment (A and B in Chart 2.3), are both "social facts." So, too, are the most important elements used in the explanation, those collected under C in Chart 2.3, as well as D, E, and F. However, some elements which presumably impact these social facts (especially E, the supply of traditional labor force participants) involve subjective states thought to be prevalent among members of various groups. For instance, the important variable I (definitions and evaluations of actor capabilities) refers to perceptions by both group members and potential employers of the employment potentials of women and minority group members. These perceptions, which are essentially stereotypes, are not individual; they are cultural and/or subcultural (i.e., group) phenomena. Nonetheless, they refer to subjective states of people. The same logic applies to element J, subcultural definitions of important and desirable work. In general, however, the assumptions which underpin this theory are rooted in the social factist paradigm.

Some of the domain assumptions which underpin our theory are:

(1) We assume that there is no biologically inherent basis for labor force inequality between groups; that women and minorities are not intrinsically incapable of doing the same jobs as white males.

(2) We assume that the rate of labor force participation and patterns of occupational deployment of the dominant social category (white males in this case) constitute the norm against which all other groups (women and racial/ethnic minorities) should be compared. The logical extension of this assumption is that "equality" exists when there is no difference in elements A and B between white males on the one hand and women and minority groups on the other. At that point the "traditional supply of labor" will include every category of people.

(3) We assume that, unless the supply of labor from the group which usually does a given job falls short of the demand, new groups cannot gain entrance. In other words, we assume inertia in employment rates and patterns unless the demand for labor and/or the supply of traditional labor force participants changes. Other possible sources of change (e.g., changing attitudes or political action) are seen as potentially important only *after* change has been initiated by the types of supply and/or demand factors specified.

42

(4) We assume that as long as there is not equality, there will always be nonemployed women and minority group members available to pull into the labor force; that there is no problem with labor supply among those who are not white males. This assumption is the opposite of that made by many who study labor force participation and occupational deployment among women. They emphasize those things that presumably impact the availability of women for work, such as how many children women have, the ages and spacing of those children, cultural factors which discourage women from working on the basis that gainful employment is unfeminine, and so forth.

(5) We assume that until equality is gained and a given group has become a part of the traditional supply of labor, changes over time can (and do) occur in both directions: toward greater similarity with the social majority on A and B and, at other times, toward greater dissimilarity. In other words, we do not assume that change is cumulative and irreversible in direction.

In assessing these assumptions, you should be aware that two of the three of us who have developed this theory have been personal recipients of employment discrimination (on the basis of sex). Moreover, the general sociopolitical and intellectual climate within which our ideas have developed must be recalled. First, the past decade has witnessed the rapid growth of social movements among women and several minority groups, all dedicated to fighting for equality between their group and white males. This struggle has helped to influence public policy so that it is now unlawful for most employers to discriminate on the basis of sex and ethnic/racial category. Simultaneously, and at least partially as a result of government policy and social movement activity, it has become less socially acceptable to hold, or at least express stereotypical and prejudicial attitudes toward women and minority groups. However, after a period of prosperity when females and minority group members made strides toward labor force equality with white males, a severe recession hit, reversing some of those gains. A high unemployment rate has brought with it pressure from some white males to reverse many federal rules and guidelines developed to end discrimination; an attack has been mounted on presumed "quotas" which, it is claimed, discriminate categorically against white males. It is within this uncertain context that the three of us have developed our ideas based on the assumptions listed.

STUDENT EXERCISES

1. Make a list of at least three assumptions you make about "human nature." Why do you make these assumptions? What would it do to your thinking about other people, yourself, and your society if, in each case, you made the opposite assumption?

2. In Exercise 2 of Chapter 2 you developed three explanations. Review them, and examine the assumptions about human beings (including yourself) implicit in each. Do the same for the explanations developed in Exercise 1, Chapter 1. Do your assumptions contradict each other? Now that you have looked more carefully at them, do you accept them? Where do you think your assumptions come from?

3. What assumptions were made about human beings and human societies by the writers of the United States Declaration of Independence and the Constitution? What are some alternative assumptions that could form the basis for a government?

CHAPTER 4

Concepts: The Building Blocks of Theories

All theories consist of symbols. In some sciences, such as physics, the symbols take the form of mathematics, a highly precise symbolic language. In sociology a few theories are now stated mathematically, but this trend is increasing, and in the future many of our theories will probably be stated in this fashion. For the present, however, the majority have been and continue to be stated in less precise form, using words as symbols. In Chapter 1 levels of abstraction were discussed. At that time the point was made that theories consist of *words that are relatively high in level of abstractness.* These types of words are called *concepts.* They comprise the building blocks and provide the content of theories. Concepts thus play a crucial role in theories and careful attention must be paid to their development and precise definition; a solid edifice cannot arise from weak, faulty, or carelessly put together building blocks.

A. The Uses and Abuses of Jargon

The primary purpose of any symbolic language is clear, precise communication. In everyday conversation we often communicate simultaneously at several levels: intellectual, emotional, evaluative, and others. This occurs because the words used in everyday language take on many meanings and, often, emotional overtones. For instance, the word "democracy" in our society usually evokes a host of positive feelings while it also conveys many things about political process and structure. Moreover, exactly what it conveys about the political world varies substantially according to the user and hearer of the word. For some it involves the right of citizens to vote periodically in elections where more than one alternative is available. To others, it involves a variety of civil rights, such as those embodied in our Bill of Rights. Still others conjure images of a representative legislature, of universal adult suffrage, and so on.

It would be very difficult, if not impossible, to do scientific work using symbols that have so many meanings and emotional states attached to them. Scientific theories that will be amendable to empirical testing require that the symbols (concepts) employed have precision of meaning; that (ideally) the user and hearer (or reader) will interpret the meaning of the symbol in identical fashion. Moreover, the emotional baggage attached to many words must be dropped if the scientist is to reach any degree of objectivity. Values and emotions should be expressed as assumptions, not as accidents associated with word usage.

The social sciences face a dilemma. Everyday language provides words which relate to virtually all of the phenomena studied by social scientists, but it does so with all the ambiguity described. There are two solutions to this dilemma: (1) use everyday words but take care to define them precisely and use them only as defined; or (2) develop new words.

Both approaches have been used in the development of sociological theory, but each presents drawbacks. In the first case, careful definition of commonly used words, there is the ever-present tendency for the user and/or the hearer (reader) to slip back into the less precise usage or to associate with it emotional or evaluative meanings. When new words are developed it often seems as if the user is simply trying to render obscure that which is very simple. The pejorative term "jargon" to refer to such technical words conveys this view. A recent Tumbleweeds cartoon made the point quite clearly when it showed an Indian chief questioning one of his braves' use of the term "peer group evaluation session" instead of "pow wow." A further problem arises from developing new words. The hearer (or reader) is constantly disrupted when trying to understand the discussion by having to recall what the newly minted vocabulary means. If the number of new terms is very large and the resultant effort required to comprehend the discussion too great, the reader (or hearer) may simply give up in frustration. The result will be a total failure to communicate rather than more precise communication. This is especially apt to happen if the reader (hearer) suspects that the ideas being expressed by the complex jargon are really quite simple and could be readily expressed in "normal" language. Finally, a problem arises from the fact that many technical words (e.g., charisma) pass into the everyday language and, in the process, lose much of their original precision. The science then faces the original dilemma of using an everyday term or developing yet a new concept until it, too, becomes popularized.

To the extent that most sociologists continue to develop theories by the use of words rather than mathematical symbols, some middle ground will have to be used. Common words with too much emotional baggage and/or a large variety of meanings will often be replaced by new terms or by words seldom used in everyday conversation (e.g., "norms," "social system," "deviant," "socialization"). This is no excuse, however, for writing or speaking in barbaric language that is unnecessarily difficult for readers (hearers) to understand in order to appear more "scientific" or "professional." For the rest, common words such as "class," "culture," "power," "society," or "group" can be used when accompanied by clear and precise definitions.

Words, as has been repeatedly pointed out, are symbols; they are not real things in themselves. For two reasons it is important to remember this. First of all, much energy is wasted when people—scientists as well as others—argue over the meaning of words. It matters little what symbol we attach to something, as long as those who are communicating understand each other. For instance, if you wish to call the thing you are reading a "book" and I wish to call it a "smertz," why argue? We are speaking of the same thing and either symbol will do. Needless to add, if we are to continue communicating it will aid the process enormously if we come to consensus on whether to call it a "book," a "smertz," or compromise by terming it a "gleeb." In sociology, we have often witnessed considerable debate that is little more fruitful than the book-smertz argument. For purposes of communication, ideally consensus should be reached among the practitioners of a given science on the use of a particular symbol. To the extent that there is such agreement, every time the word is used it will mean the same thing and whenever that thing is meant, that word will be used. This is often not the case in

47

sociology. Concepts such as "social class" and "role," for instance, have many different definitions which may be only subtly different or may be widely disparate in meaning. For other concepts, such as "norm" and "socialization" there is widespread consensus of meaning. If you examine closely the intellectual arguments you as well as many sociologists get into, you will find that often they are no more than debates over word usage, not over substantive issues.

There is a second important reason to remember that words are nothing more or less than symbols or abstractions. *When we treat our abstractions as if they were real things, we are guilty of reification.* In Chapter 2, some criticisms of sociological theories which include a notion of equilibrium were discussed. Theorists who incorporate the idea of equilibrium into a systems analysis are often reasoning by analogy, whether consciously or not. The human body is a system; it has equilibrating mechanisms. Society is a social system; therefore, by analogy with the body, it too has equilibrating mechanisms. The analogy does not hold, however, because the concept "social system" has been reified in this approach. A human body is real, tangible, perceivable by the senses. A social system is an abstraction; it is not tangible or perceivable by the senses. Reification leads, in this case, to the development of a theory rooted in an untenable analogy. The problem of reification is ever present in sociology because many of our concepts are abstractions with no one-to-one relationship to "real," concrete phenomena. They are useful in helping us to understand and explain concrete phenomena, but they must not be treated as real in their own right. Concepts such as "group," "community," and "social class" are very easy to reify.

B. DEFINITIONS

It should be clear from the preceding section that good theory depends on good definitions of the concepts involved. In everyday life we often define words for others. We do so with more or less precision, care, and self-consciousness. This section should aid you in rendering clearer and more precise definitions by becoming more self-conscious about what you are doing.

The two simplest means of defining words are not normally very useful for theory construction. As young children we learn the meaning of a word, or the word that is attached to something, by *ostensive definition*. *Ostensive definitions consist of demonstrating the meaning of a word in a nonverbal fashion.* When, for instance, a child asks "What's a book?" the parents will point to one or several objects which are normally called books. Ostensive definitions may be useful for the beginning stages of a research project, but they are not useful in theory construction. In the former case a researcher may have a rather vague idea which cannot be defined, but examples of which can be pointed out. The researcher would then examine the examples carefully in an attempt to develop a definition which is not ostensive (Zetterberg, 1965, p. 35). For instance, someone may be unable to define "creativity" but can point to individuals who appear to be creative. By studying those individuals the researcher may be able to pinpoint the attribute "creativity" and subsequently develop a verbal definition for it. Since theories are typically communicated via printed media, however, ostensive definitions have little utility in their construction. Occasionally a picture might be employed as an ostensive definition, but this is rare in the behavioral and social sciences.

All definitions which are not ostensive are verbal definitions; they employ words. The simplest verbal definition is a synonym, namely, another word (presumably known already to the hearer or reader) which means the same thing as the one in question. Earlier in this book I defined "stochastic" as synonymous with "probabilistic" on the assumption that you were already acquainted with the latter term. Synonyms are not very useful in theory construction because, if a single, well-known word exists which covers the meaning intended, why bother to use a different one? In this case, a new or obscure word would often constitute jargon for its own sake.

This leaves us with having to define our concepts verbally by using several words to convey, as precisely as possible, the meaning intended. Probably the best means available to avoid a major problem often encountered in definitions (to be discussed below) is to employ the age-old form developed by Aristotle. An *Aristotelian definition* consists of two parts. The first part, called the *genus proximum*, tells what the phenomenon in question shares with a larger class of phenomena. The second part, the *genus specifica*, tells what is peculiar to the phenomenon in question. What is "deviance?" Human actions *(genus proximum)* which are nonnormative *(genus specifica)*. What are Moslems? People who adhere to a set of religious beliefs *(genus proximum)* based on the teachings of Mohammed as written in the Koran *(genus specifica)*.

Another type of verbal definition consists of simply enumerating a series of other, previously defined concepts which, collectively, define the one in question (Zetterberg, 1965, p. 40). This is a common practice in sociology. For instance, one definition of "social class" (a Marxian one) is: a category of people who stand in the same relationship to the ownership of the means of production (i.e., they are either owners or non-owners) *and* whose members are aware of their communality of interests in opposition to those of the other social class. Another definition of "social class" might read: a category of people who share in common approximately equal occupational prestige, income, *and* education. In the first definition two attributes are listed, in the second three, all of which are either previously defined or presumed to be understood by the hearer (reader).

This commonly utilized form of definition is weak. To understand why requires further discussion of the nature of definitions. Earlier it was pointed out that words are no more or less than symbols arbitrarily attached to meanings we wish to convey; any symbol will do as long as the communicators agree to use it to cover a given meaning. What this means is that definitions cannot be "true" or "false" statements; they are only statements of how a concept will be used. To say that "deviance" means nonnormative behavior does not imply anything about reality. It is not a statement that one can say is true or false. It is no more than a means of pinning a label on something. To say that a social class consists of people who share two or three attributes in common, however, can suggest something about the real world: that the attributes used in the definition commonly occur together (e.g., that people with high occupational prestige tend to have high income and education). In this case the statement can be "true" or "false." This type of definition, in short, goes beyond pinning a label on something to assert something about the empirical world. Zetterberg called such definitions *"truth-asserting" definitions* (1965, pp. 37-41). In Chapter 6 you will find that it is the function of propositions and hypotheses to assert something about empirical reality. It is not the function of definitions to do so. Truth-asserting definitions are thus, in reality, hypotheses or propositions, not definitions. However, because they are treated as definitions, their real nature is often obscured. This means that assumptions about reality are "smuggled" into the theory through the definitions.

There is one further type of definition, called an *operational definition,* which is of crucial importance to social scientists. However, its importance is primarily to the research endeavor, not to theory construction, and as such it will be discussed later in this chapter.

C. THE INTER-RELATIONS OF DEFINITIONS

The words which constitute sociological theories are of different types. Zetterberg (1965, pp. 43-57) presents the following scheme to depict the types of words used in theories:

    I. Logical words
   II. Extralogical words
      1. Primitive terms
         a. Minimum terms
         b. Borrowed terms
      2. Derived terms (p. 50)

Logical words are shared by all sciences and provide the connectives in a theory. Such words as "and," "or," "equal to," "increase," and so on are logical terms. The exact role played by such terms will be explored further in Chapter 6. They are, of course, not necessary to define in presenting a theory.

Extralogical words are all those terms which provide the content for the particular theory. They, therefore, tend to be specific to a science, or sometimes to a theory within one science. All the sociological terms you learn (e.g., "norm," "role," "social structure," "socialization," "group") are extralogical words. These are the concepts that require definition in developing and presenting a theory. Zetterberg's scheme shows that there are several different kinds of extralogical words.

Primitive terms are those extralogical words which are defined in their own right. Derived terms are those which are defined by reference to the primitive terms. In short, theories consist of extralogical concepts whose definitions often build upon one another and thus come to comprise a system of interrelated concepts. For instance, Max Weber (1947, pp. 152-153) defined "power" in terms of the ability to get others to do as one wills, regardless of whether or not they wish to. "Legitimacy" is defined in terms of people obeying a person or group because of the belief that the person or group has the right to be obeyed and thus others have the moral obligation to obey. These concepts,

51

"power" and "legitimacy," which are in this case primitive terms, are then combined to define the derived term "authority": authority is legitimated power.

The final distinction made by Zetterberg is between two types of primitive terms. Concepts may be unique to a given science, in which case they are called *minimum terms,* or they may be borrowed from another discipline, in which case they are called *borrowed terms.* An example of a minimum term in sociology is "norm," while "stratum," which was taken from geology, is a borrowed term.

The distinction between minimum and borrowed terms is important for at least two reasons. First, as Zetterberg rightfully argues (1965, pp. 50-52), a science which has no minimum terms is not a separate science. If all of the concepts employed come from another field then there is no rationale for calling the field a separate science. From this perspective, much of the work of the great early sociologists (e.g., Durkheim, Weber) can be seen as efforts to develop concepts which included minimum terms so as to establish sociology as a science separate and distinct in its own right.

The second reason the distinction is important is that it sensitizes theorists to the risk of employing borrowed terms. Concepts have meanings within a given paradigm and often a specific theoretical context. If one borrows a concept, it is very easy to borrow assumptions unwittingly from the original context. In this instance one ends up arguing by analogy and, as we saw earlier when discussing the concept "equilibrium," the analogy may be inappropriate. The message here is that extreme care is needed when using borrowed terms to ensure that unwarranted assumptions are not simultaneously and unconsciously "smuggled" into the theory. To give another example, the concept "stratum" or "strata" is borrowed from geology. Geologic strata can be physically identified as different from one another; they directly reflect "real" entities. Sociological strata are abstractions; they are arbitrary dividing lines placed on a continuum of differences and, as such, are neither "real" nor tangibly identifiable. It would not be hard, however, to create theories that reify the sociological concept if our mental image of the term includes the geologic usage.

D. OPERATIONALIZING CONCEPTS

From the very outset of this book stress has been placed on the necessity of relating theory to research (and vice versa). In order to do this, the abstract concepts upon which theories are built must be rendered in a form that is amenable to observation and measurement in concrete cases. In the research endeavor theoretical concepts are converted to observable *variables* which are given *operational definitions*.

The term "variable" has been used occasionally earlier in the book, along with words such as "element" and "phenomenon," which have been employed as loose synonyms for "variable." It is time now to get more precise in our use of the term. *A variable is anything that can be measured empirically and can take on different values* (i.e., varies). Income is a variable, as are homicide rate, age, population density, IQ test scores, sex, and religion. *Things which cannot take on different values are called constants.* The concepts used in theories also refer to phenomena which vary, but they cannot be observed and measured directly until they are converted to variables.

Variables are given *operational definitions. An operational definition is one in which the word (variable) is defined in terms of how it is measured in a given research effort.* For instance, a definition of the variable "sex role preference" might be the score on a standard sex role inventory test. "Intelligence" can be defined operationally as the score on an IQ test, "interaction" as the number of times people in a given group speak directly to one another in a specified time period. To do research all variables must be operationalized, that is, means (also called *research instruments)* must be developed to measure them, and these constitute the operational definitions.

To the extent that research and theory are to be related to one another, care needs to be given to the ways in which abstract concepts and their definitions are related to variables and their operationalizations. This issue is called *validity. Validity refers to the degree to which that which is being measured corresponds to that which the scientist thinks is being measured,* namely, the concept.

Perfect validity would mean that the measurement instrument measured everything meant by the concept and nothing else. This is relatively rare in sociology. The worst possible case is that in which the operationalization measures nothing meant by the concept (for example, if one measured the concept "intelligence" with a thermometer!). Hopefully, that rarely if ever occurs either.

There are two forms of less-than-perfect validity that are typical in sociology. The first is quite acceptable: the instrument (operationalization) measures only some part of the concept but nothing else. An example of this would be employing rape, burglary, and theft rates to measure the concept "crime rates." Nothing that is not covered by "crime rates" is measured, but many other things included in the concept (e.g., rates of assault, homicide, forgery) are omitted. This procedure is acceptable (especially if resources prevent a more complete study), since another research project could be conducted using those types of rates excluded in this instance.

The second form of less-than-perfect validity is to be avoided whenever possible, although it is not unusual to find it in sociology. In this instance, the operationalization includes some things not meant by the concept along with things that are meant. An example of this would occur if we developed a measurement of marital happiness that accidentally also tapped job satisfaction. Another example of this type of partial validity are aptitude tests which also measure achievement. Well-defined concepts and research instruments are *unidimensional,* that is, *they mean or measure only one dimension of a phenomenon.* Operationalizations which suffer from this form of nonvalidity lack unidimensionality; they measure more than one thing. It is often difficult to know when an instrument lacks unidimensionality. Such techniques as factor analysis and Guttman scaling, when they are usable, can aid in the identification and development of unidimensional research instruments. A discussion of these research techniques, along with others involved in assessing validity, are, however, beyond the scope of this primer.

Just as concepts and their definitions are of different types, so are variables and their operationizations. First of all, in sociology there are two very different types of variables, one referring to individual phenomena and one to group or aggregate phenomena. Confusion of these types causes serious problems. When data are collected from and presented in terms of individuals, we have the former; when they are collected from or presented in terms of aggregates of people, or corporate actors such as nations or associations, we have the latter. The same concept may be involved in either case, however, and this is what often causes problems. For instance, the Census Bureau collects data from individuals on a large number of variables (e.g., age, education, income, occupation). It publishes this data in group or aggregate form (e.g., the median or average age, education, income, etc., in geographic areas called census tracts). If *conclusions about individuals are drawn on the basis of aggregate or group data* (a not uncommon occurrence), we have a case of what is called the *ecological fallacy*. In committing the ecological fallacy misleading conclusions may be drawn. For instance, data on voting behavior are often aggregate data based on voting precincts. Suppose we had two precincts: Precinct A is 75 percent white and voted 75 percent Republican; Precinct B is 75 percent black and voted 75 percent Democratic. You could draw the conclusion that whites vote Republican and blacks Democratic. If you did, however, you would be committing the ecological fallacy, since you are drawing conclusions concerning the manner in which individuals vote on the basis of grouped data. It is possible, for instance, that all the blacks in precinct A voted Republican and all the whites in B voted Democratic. To say anything accurate about who voted how in each precinct, data on color and vote would have to be collected (usually by a survey) from individuals within the two precincts. Often, conclusions presented in the mass media are based on group data which have been analyzed and reported in such a way that the ecological fallacy has been committed.

The second way in which variables may be classified is according to whether they are continuous or categorical (comprised of categories). A continuous variable is one in which the values which can be taken range along a continuum bounded by a maximum and a minimum. Income is a continuous variable ranging from zero to whatever amount the richest person receives. There are values at every meaningful point in between (e.g., $10,572.31; $15,621.42). Similarly, age, occupational prestige, IQ scores are all continuous variables. Variables which are not continuous are comprised of categories. Political party preference ("Democrat," "Republican," "Independent") is one example of this type of variable, as are marital status and types of crimes. Continuous variables may be made into categorical variables. If, instead of treating age as a continuum from one day to the age of the oldest person in the population, you created age categories, you would be converting this continuous variable to a categorical variable. We might thus have "infancy" (up to eighteen months), "toddler" (eighteen months and a day to four years), "young child" (four years and a day to eight years), "older child" (eight years and a day to twelve), and so on. These categories could be made quite detailed (as I just did) or fairly broad (e.g., "child," "adolescent," "young adult," "middle aged," "elderly").

There is a third way in which variables may be divided into different types, namely, according to the *level of measurement*. There are four levels of measurement available, regardless of the science involved. For each level certain statistical procedures are appropriate. As one goes higher in the levels, the statistics appropriate to lower levels may be used plus others which cannot be used with lower levels. Thus, it is desirable to use the highest level possible. The statistics appropriate to each level will not, however, be discussed in this book.

The lowest is called the *nominal level* of measurement. In this instance *the values which may be taken by the variable cannot be ranked as higher or lower than one another, only different.* Thus, the variable "sex" has two values, male and female, which are different but not amenable to saying that one is more than or less than the other. Many of the major variables in sociology are nominal, (e.g., religious preference, marital status, political party preference).

The remaining three levels of measurement all involve ranking of the values taken by the variable. In order from lowest to highest they are *ordinal, interval,* and *ratio. In ordinal measurement the values are rank ordered, but one cannot say that the intervals between each rank are equal.* An example of ordinal measurement might be a scale of religiosity that asked respondents to indicate how religious they consider themselves, ranging from "very religious" to "somewhat religious" to "slightly religious" to "not at all religious." Someone who is "somewhat religious" is more so than the person who answered "slightly" so and less so than the person who answered "very religious." However, we cannot conclude that the person who answered "very religious" is the same amount more religious than the person answering "slightly" as she or he is less religious than the person who said "very religious."

The next highest level of measurement, *the interval level, is reached when the intervals between rankings are equal, but there is no absolute zero.* Because there is no absolute zero, we cannot say that someone who scores 50 is twice as much as someone who scores 25. The Fahrenheit (and also Celsius) thermometer is an everyday example of an interval scale. The difference between 10° and 11° is identical to the difference between 25° and 26°. However, since zero is an arbitrary point on this scale, we do not say that 50° is twice as hot as 25°. Many sociological scales are treated as if they are interval measures despite a lack of firm evidence that the intervals between values are indeed equal (e.g., scales of occupational prestige, various attitude scales). This gives the

56

appearance that the information presented is more precise than in fact it is.

The highest level of measurement, *the ratio scale, has an absolute or real zero point along with equal intervals between ranked values.* Rates of social phenomena (e.g., arrest rates, suicide rates, birth rates) and income are examples of a ratio scale. Not only is the difference between $2,000 and $3,000 equal to the difference between $150,000 and $151,000, but $4,000 is twice as much money as $2,000 because $0 is a meaningful number. However, in another sense income, age, and many other seemingly ratio scales are only ordinal scales when used by sociologists. While a fifty-year-old has lived twice as many days as a twenty-five-year-old, developmentally one year is not equal to another year regardless of where in the life cycle it occurs. The amount of change which occurs between ages two and three is not the same as that which occurs between thirty-three and thirty-four. Similarly, the meaning of an additional $1,000 is quite different when added to an income of $3,000 compared to $50,000. It is not usually age or income per se that is of interest to sociologists but the meaning or ramifications of these variables to people. In this sense, they are not ratio scales.

Thus, despite the fact that sociologists employ ratio and interval scales, in terms of the meanings of our measurements and our ability to prove equidistance between values, most sociological scales (with the exception of rates of various phenomena) are in fact ordinal or nominal. In short, we measure many of our variables with considerably less precision than we sometimes think we do.

Before leaving this discussion of operationalizing concepts, one final problem needs to be discussed briefly, namely, *reliability. Reliability refers to the stable functioning of the research instrument* and is thus fundamental to doing accurate research. If, for instance you stepped on a bathroom scale and got a reading, stepped off, immediately stepped back on and got a different reading, you would have an unreliable scale. You know that in that time period your weight didn't change, and you therefore conclude that your scale isn't working properly. You would reach the same conclusion if you and a friend, known to weigh the same amount as you, received different readings from your scale. It is usually a somewhat more complex matter to determine whether or not sociological instruments are reliable, but the issue is the same. A number of techniques have been developed to aid this process; however, a discussion of them is beyond the scope of this book. The important thing to understand in this context is that without a reliable instrument there can be no validity, and therefore no theory testing. The opposite, however, is not necessarily the case; you can have reliability without validity. An instrument may function stably but not measure what you want it to. It measures nothing if it is not stable (i.e., reliable).

E. EXEMPLAR

The time has come to explore the meanings and some possible operationalizations of the concepts on Chart 2.3 which comprise our theory. Each concept (i.e., boxed expression) will be taken in turn and first defined verbally and then a suggested approach to operationalization will be presented.

(A) Rate of Labor Force Participation: The proportion of a category of people (e.g., females, blacks, white males) which is gainfully employed (i.e., work for wages or salaries) at a given time. The measurement will be secondhand: data on employment collected and disseminated by the Bureau of Labor Statistics and/or the Census Bureau, both agencies of the United States government.

(B) Occupational Deployment: The pattern of dispersal, throughout the range of jobs within the society, characteristic of a category of employed people. Measurement is based on same sources as A above.

(C.1) Level of Technology: The extent to which a society and/or particular industry relies upon tools and machines rather than human muscle to produce goods and services. This is operationalized by measuring worker productivity, or how much output is produced per unit (e.g., hour, day, week) of human labor time.

(C.2) State of Economy: The extent to which prosperity (or recession) characterizes all sectors of the economy of a society. Measurement of this variable would employ some or all of the many indicators used by economists and collected by the government, such as rates of investment, overall unemployment rates, and so on.

(C.3) Availability of Natural Resources: The extent to which available supplies of nonhuman resources (e.g., petroleum, various minerals) are adequate to meet commercial and industrial demand. Operationalization consists of business-reported shortages of any needed resources.

(C.4) Population Size and Structure: The total number of people in a society and the distribution of those people by age categories. These data are provided by the United States Bureau of Census.

(D) Demand for Labor: The number of workers sought for any given type of occupation and/or the total number sought for all occupations in a society at any one time. This could be operationalized by carefully sampling a number of employers and asking what job openings are available in their companies. State employment commissions often accumulate such data.

(E) Supply of Traditional Labor Force Participants: The number of members of the category of people who predominate in a given occupation (e.g., females in nursing or secretarial work, white males in engineering or business management) who are trained and available for employment in that occupation. This variable might be operationalized by sampling a cross section of people who are not employed in the labor force to determine their skills and desire for employment.

(F) Demand for Nontraditional Labor Force Participation: The extent to which the supply of traditional labor force participants is inadequate to meet the demand for labor. This derived term is operationalized by subtracting E from D; if the result is positive (i.e., D is greater than E), then there is a demand for nontraditional labor force participants; otherwise there is not.

(G) Traditional Labor Force Influence: The extent to which members of a traditional labor force group collectively attempt to retain their position in the labor market *vis-à-vis* other groups by use of organized tactics (e.g., union restrictions, impact on governmental policy). Measurement of this variable would be very imprecise. One could examine who opposes legislation at the state and federal levels that support the employment opportunities of various nontraditional groups (e.g., what groups fund the anti-ERA movement or oppose civil rights legislation). One could also examine union and professional association policies related to entrance requirements for possible bias against various groups.

(H) Vocational-Career Planning: The extent to which members of various categories of people go about acquiring the education and skills necessary to a particular occupation. This could be operationalized by examining the characteristics (gender, race, and ethnicity) of a sample of those enrolled in a large variety of educational and vocational programs at all levels from high school on (e.g., business schools, nursing programs, engineering colleges, high school mechanics, drafting programs, data processing programs).

(I) Definitions and Evaluations of Actor Capabilities: The extent to which the members of a given category of people are defined by employers and/or by themselves as capable (or incapable) of performing various employment tasks. This concept refers to social stereotypes about groups and the abilities of group members. Its operationalization could be based on one of the standard measures of social stereotypes given as questionnaires to samples of employers and group members. This variable may prove not to be unidimensional in which case the various dimensions (e.g., employers' stereotypes and group member stereotypes) would have to be separated.

(J) Subcultural Definitions of Important and Desirable Work: The extent to which members of a category of people define any given occupation as one to which it is worthy to aspire or honorable to perform. Questionnaire items which tap subjective appraisals of a large number of occupations could be given to samples of different categories of people.

(K) Lack of Alternatives: The extent to which members of a given category of people are barred through discrimination from gaining entrance into a number of occupations, especially those of relatively high prestige and/or income. Since employment discrimination on the basis of sex, race, and ethnicity is illegal, its form has become subtle and very difficult to document and measure. If we were to employ as a measure of this variable the often used approach of examining the extent to which a given group is underrepresented in a given occupation (i.e., whether there is a smaller proportion of members employed in that field than lives in the society at large), we would render our model tautological. Since one of the variables we are attempting to explain is precisely the extent to which various groups are underrepresented in given occupations (Variable B), if we measure another variable in the same way, we are engaged in circular reasoning and, therefore, create a tautology. Some form of questioning group members on their hiring and promotion experiences would be necessary to attempt to discover whether or not they perceived discrimination on the basis of group membership. This is, at best, a very rough approximation of the concept, since perceptions of discrimination may be very incongruent with the reality of discrimination (i.e., people may perceive discrimination when it did not occur or fail to see it when it did).

(L) Social Movement Activity: The extent to which members of a category organize to pursue greater equity for (i.e., less discrimination and stereotyping against) that group. Again, operationalization of this variable, like E, involves hunting for any evidence of such organized activity. Given the contemporary media, it is likely that the existence of an organized movement will not long escape some degree of public notice.

(M) Political and Legal Policy: The extent to which laws are passed, executive orders are issued, and court decisions are rendered which affect (positively or adversely) the employment rights and opportunities of a category of people. A search through the records of state and federal court decisions, executive orders, and legislation (all of which are regularly published) will provide this information.

The concepts which have been employed in this model are of a relatively low level of abstraction. Problems which arise in operationalizing them occur mostly because of the wide scope of data needed, but validity problems are minimized because of the relatively concrete nature of the concepts employed. Many of the terms are borrowed from other social sciences, especially economics; others are minimum terms (I, J, and L especially). Thus, this theory is not, strictly speaking, a purely sociological one. Rather, it is interdisciplinary in focus. The levels of measurement which would probably be employed include the ratio level (e.g., variables A, B, D), the ordinal level (e.g., G, J), and the nominal level (e.g., I). The variables could all be operationalized independently of one another, thus avoiding tautology. The various categories of people are treated simply as statistical entities (unless they organize themselves as groups as in variables G and L) thus avoiding reification. The ecological fallacy is avoided because the conclusions to be drawn on the basis of aggregate data pertain to aggregates, not individuals. We trust that we have avoided creating jargon for its own sake and that the definitions provided are not truth-asserting.

STUDENT EXERCISES

1. List as many possible usages, definitions and/or synonyms as you can think of for each of the following. Also, specify the emotional states each might evoke when used in this country.

   a. Fascist
   b. Black
   c. Capitalism
   d. Class
   e. Culture
2. Develop an Aristotelian definition for each of the following and specify the *genus proximum* and *genus specifica* in each definition:
   a. Community
   b. Folkway
   c. Juvenile delinquent
   d. Peer group
   e. Immigration
3. For each of the following give an Aristotelian definition and then attempt one operational definition. Discuss the problem of validity for each.
   a. Geographical mobility
   b. Family cohesiveness
   c. Racial stereotype
   d. Intergroup conflict
4. For each of the following, what is the level of measurement? Justify your answer.
   a. IQ test scores (ranging from 0 to about 180)
   b. Race (black, white, Oriental, native American, other)
   c. Frequency of movie going (daily, weekly, monthly, yearly, less often)
   d. Examination grades, based on percentages
   e. Examination grades, based on letter grades

CHAPTER **5**

Classification Schemes: More Building Blocks of Theories

In the last chapter, concepts were discussed without making a clear distinction between those which are unidimensional and those which are multidimensional. Indeed, at one stage the point was made that concepts *ought* to be unidimensional. By and large, the most useful concepts for theory construction and testing are unidimensional (Hage, 1972, Chapter 1). However, there are times when more complex types of concepts, which refer to multidimensional categories rather than single dimensions, are useful. These *more complex concepts will be called classifications.* An example of this distinction can be seen when we examine the concept "democracy," which may be seen as one value of a variable theoretical concept "types of political structure." The term "democracy" is multidimensional and includes phenomena of political structure (e.g., elected legislative bodies), political process (e.g., voting among alternative candidates), possibly political culture (e.g., valuing political and legal equality), and so on. This multidimensional concept could, however, be broken down into a series of unidimensional ones: the extent to which political decisions are made by elected representatives, the extent to which voters are provided with real alternatives among which to choose, the extent to which citizens value political and legal equality.

A. The Uses and Abuses of Classification

The words employed by people both reflect their reality and shape their perceptions of reality. Snow is a very important component of the reality of Eskimos; they have a large number of different words to distinguish among different types of snow. In turn, armed with this rich vocabulary, Eskimos are able to perceive subtleties of snow lost to those who live in warmer climates and lack the relevant vocabulary. In short, it is difficult to perceive that for which we lack concepts, and we are sensitized to that for which we have a rich vocabulary. In this characteristic, science in no way differs from everyday life.

Many phenomena of social life are highly complex (e.g., bureaucracy, types of political systems, types of societies). When rendered into a series of unidimensional concepts, the complex web of the whole may be lost to the perception of the investigator; the individual trees are seen more clearly, but not the forest. Conversely, however, broad classification of the whole may blind one to the workings of the parts; the forest is visible, but the trees are indistinguishable. Thus, a science of social life requires both unidimensional concepts and multidimensional classifications, and the determination of which will be employed will be based on the purpose for which the concept is to be used.

Many, if not most classifications are time- and/or space-specific; they are not found in all societies and/or all historical epochs. Examples include "peasant society," "feudalism," "fascism," "caste," and "bureaucracy." When used, therefore, there is always the risk that the similarities between two phenomena separated by time and/or space will be missed because the dissimilarities prevent the use of the same general label. Thus, if the scientist is seeking to understand universal phenomena, she or he is better off using unidimensional concepts. If, however, the goal is to describe or understand in depth a (relatively) unique phenomenon, the multidimensional concept is appropriate.

By and large social science theory represents an effort to understand universal rather than historically specific phenomena. To the extent that this is true, as Hage (1972) points out, we need to employ unidimensional variables rather than complex classifications. What, then, are the appropriate uses for the latter? Clearly, historians use the latter quite

64

often; they are primarily concerned with unique events, structures, and processes. In short, classifications are rich in descriptive, if not analytical or explanatory potential, and detailed description is a central task of history. It is, however, also a task of social scientists, who are not solely and exclusively theoreticians.

Classifications can be especially helpful in the early stages of research. We may, for instance, have a clear impression that rural societies are different from urban, that bureaucratic organizations are different from primary groups, that democracy is a very different political system from totalitarianism. What we may lack is a precise set of dimensions which can be treated as separate variables. The process of developing a classification may help to pinpoint such a set of unidimensional concepts. Thus, classification is not an end in itself, although some "theorists" in sociology have treated it as such. Rather, it can serve as the first step in the further development of concepts more appropriate to theory construction and testing.

There are many theories in sociology which attempt to explain a multidimensional phenomenon. Durkheim's theory explaining the evolution from societies based predominantly on "mechanical solidarity" to those based predominantly on "organic solidarity" (1893), and Weber's theory concerning the rise of the "spirit of capitalism" (1958b) are examples taken from major classics in sociology. These theories are, indeed, attempts to explain the occurrence of complex, nonuniversal phenomena. Such theories can be valuable in their own right, as explanations of time- and/or space-specific phenomena, or they may be viewed as important first efforts in the long-term development of universally applicable theories.

B. General Rules of Classification

To this point, classifications have been treated as single categories. They are, in fact, values of variables. The complex category "democracy" is one value of the normal variable "types of political systems," which might also include "authoritarian," "totalitarian," or other labels. At the very least, each complex category represents one of two values; for instance, an organization can be a bureaucracy or a "nonbureaucracy." In other words, the term used to cover a complex phenomenon is not a constant; there are other forms of the same general thing, even if the only other term is the negative of the one employed. Given this attribute, it is apparent that variables which have as their values multidimensional concepts (classifications) are nominal in their level of measurement.

The type of variable that includes complex concepts as its values will henceforth be called a classification scheme. There are two fundamental rules that apply to all classification schemes. Indeed, they apply to the operationalization of all variables, irrespective of type. These are the principles of all-inclusiveness and mutual exclusiveness of the values which comprise the variable.

The values of a variable, including classification schemes, must be *all-inclusive*. This means that *there exists a value or category that can accommodate every possible case in the real world.* For instance, the variable "marital status" must include not only the married and those never married; it needs to accommodate the legal statuses of divorced, widowed, and separated. To insure that the principle of all-inclusiveness is met, a residual category is often added to the values. *A residual category is a value which includes all other, unspecified cases.* It may be termed "other," as in a question asking religion and offering the alternatives: "none," "Protestant," "Catholic," "Jewish," "other." It may simply be a negative: one value is "bureaucratic" and the other, residual category is "non-bureaucratic." Another way to insure all-inclusiveness is to include an open-ended category. If, for instance, we were to make categories out of the continuous variable income, we could not have as our highest income level "$50,000-$100,000"; there are people whose income is greater. Therefore, our last category might be "$50,000 and over."

The second basic rule in the development of classification schemes and the operationalization of all variables is the principle of *mutual exclusiveness*. This means that *every case in the real world fits only one category*. If, for instance, we had the age categories "0-5" and "5-10," where would a five-year-old go? The appropriate categories in this case would be "0-5 years" and "6-10 years." When complex classifications are used, it is often very difficult to define categories that are mutually exclusive. For instance, if "urban society" is defined in terms of five attributes, and "rural society" is defined as being the opposite of these same five attributes, there will be numerous cases where a given society, on any one or more of these five variables, will fall somewhere in the middle. Where does one place such societies? One could add a residual category called "intermediate types." Alternatively, one could reconceptualize this classification scheme and create either an ideal type or a taxonomy. Both of these will be discussed below.

A classification scheme that conforms to the two rules of mutual exclusiveness and all-inclusiveness is one in which every relevant phenomenon in the world can be placed in one but only one category. In order to be able to do this when creating classification schemes, the attributes which constitute the complex concepts must be very clearly and precisely defined. Since, as we saw earlier, classification schemes are often developed because of an inability to define the central attributes precisely, this is often not possible. Thus, many classification schemes do not conform exactly to the canons set forth.

C. TAXONOMIES

A taxonomy is a classification scheme which is developed systematically by specifying a series of attributes and creating categories that exhaust the logical combinations of those attributes. When done consistently and properly, the resulting categories conform to the two rules discussed above. This is an exercise in logic as well as sociology and as such may result in categories for which no known examples exist in the real world. Indeed, one of the major benefits of this type of exercise is to alert a scientist to a logically possible phenomenon so that he or she can make a special effort to find a case in which it does exist. In other words, the scientist may be alerted to a relatively rare phenomenon that might otherwise be missed or ignored. Failure to find such a case is itself important inasmuch as it raises theoretical questions concerning why it does not exist.

William Kornhauser has developed a relatively simple taxonomy that can serve as an example (1959, p. 40). His taxonomy refers to types of political systems. He specifies two attributes: availability of nonelites and accessibility of elites. He defines the first as "the extent to which members of the society lack attachments to independent groups" (i.e., groups independent of the government). The second is defined by Kornhauser as "the extent to which members of the society participate in the selection of elites" (i.e., of those who actually govern). He then dichotomizes each attribute into two values, "high" and "low." Clearly, use of this taxonomy in actual research would necessitate precise instructions concerning the cutoff points which distinguish high from low in both attributes, as well as operational definitions of each attribute. His taxonomy looks like this (1959, p. 40):

Availability of Nonelites

		Low	High
Accessibility of Elites	Low	Communal Society	Totalitarian Society
	High	Pluralist Society	Mass Society

Presumably, every society could be measured according to the two variables and, therefore, find its place in one of the four categories which comprise the values of this classification scheme or taxonomy. Subsequently, questions could be asked concerning other attributes of societies which might cause them to be of one type or another and/or result from the various types. One important point should be noted: the definition of each of the four types is given by its position within the taxonomy. For instance, a "mass society" is defined as one in which there is high accessibility of elites and high availability of nonelites. All other possible attributes are considered correlates, not part of the definition, of "mass society."

Taxonomies can consist of many more than two dimensions (attributes) and/or more than two values for each. Each arithmetic increase, however, results in a geometric increase in the total number of categories in the classification scheme (taxonomy). Thus, a three-attribute taxonomy, each with only two values, would result in eight categories (2 x 2 x 2), compared to only four in the two-by-two. Clearly, the numbers become quickly unmanageable.

Many classification schemes in sociology look like taxonomies but do not fully follow the canons of logic. The result is a hodgepodge of categories, some logically derived and others totally ad hoc. Chart 5.1 presents a rather well-known scheme developed by William Petersen (1958) to classify types of migrations. Without going into detail about the meanings of his various attributes or categories, one can, nonetheless, clearly see the ad hoc nature of some of his categories. Several lines which divide different migration types begin, and in one case end, in the

CHART 5.1 PETERSON'S TYPOLOGY OF MIGRATION

Type of Interaction	Migratory Force	Class of Migration	Type of Migration	
			Conservative	Innovating
Nature and Man	Ecological Push	Primitive	Wandering / Ranging	Flight from the Land
State and Man	Migration Policy	Impelled	Flight	Coolie Trade
		Forced	Displacement	Slave Trade
Man and His Norms	Higher Aspirations	Free	Group	Pioneer
Collective Behavior	Social Momentum	Mass	Settlement	Urbanization

middle of the taxonomy. For instance, one is left questioning on what basis "wandering" is distinguished from "ranging." Similarly, how do coolie and slave trade differ, given the attributes listed at the margins of the taxonomy?

Another famous example of an inconsistent taxonomy is Merton's Typology of Modes of Individual Adaptation, shown in Chart 5.2 (1957, p. 140). Again without going into detail about the meaning of the various attributes, it is visually possible to see that there is an ad hoc category. The logically possible combinations of plusses and minuses are exhausted in the first four modes of adaptation. Mode V, Rebellion, represents Merton's sociological understanding that another type exists that is not handled within the logic of his scheme. Chances are, a third and even fourth attribute, in addition to the acceptance or rejection of cultural goals and institutionalized means, were needed in the first place in order to account for rebellion. To accommodate three attributes, Merton would have needed eight modes of adaptation, for four attributes sixteen modes.

Properly constructed, taxonomies aid in more systematic thinking, in

69

CHART 5.2 MERTON'S TYPOLOGY OF MODES OF INDIVIDUAL ADAPTATION

Modes of Adaptation	Cultural Goals	Institutionalized Means
I. Conformity	+	+
II. Innovation	+	-
III. Ritualism	-	+
IV. Retreatism	-	-
V. Rebellion	±	±

research, and in theorizing. The fact that two highly respected sociologists were unable to maintain the consistency necessary to develop logically, as well as sociologically, complete taxonomies suggests that the process is far more difficult than is apparent on the surface.

D. IDEAL AND CONSTRUCTED TYPES

Sociologists have, since the inception of the discipline, developed complex classifications called types, to aid in theory building and, probably more importantly, research. *A type is a listing of attributes which, collectively, define the phenomenon (classification) in question.* Types often occur in pairs, each part of which is presumed to be the opposite of the other (called *polar types*). Even if the polar opposite is not specified, it is often implicit as a residual category representing the opposite of the type presented. Well-known examples of polar types include Tönnies' Gemeinschaft and Gesellschaft societies (1887) and Durkheim's Mechanical and Organic types of social solidarity (1893). Weber's type of bureaucracy (1958a) exemplifies the case in which the opposite (a "non-bureaucracy") is implicit and residual. Often, the types are seen as the extreme end points on a continuum, such as Redfield's Folk-Urban Continuum (1941). Sometimes, too, more than two types are developed, such as Sorokin's three cultural types: Sensate, Ideational, and Idealistic (1937-1941). In this case, however, the middle type is a combination of attributes from two polar types and thus the three may be seen as end and midpoints on a continuum.

Types may be created by one of two fundamentally different processes. *A constructed type is one in which, based on the study of many examples of the phenomenon in question, a list of attributes which represent those most often found in reality is formed.* The list thus represents an averaging process. For instance, if one wished to create a constructed type to define "democracy," one would examine several political units known as democracies. The structures and processes found to exist most frequently would comprise the defining attributes of the type.

The second approach is to construct what Max Weber labeled an ideal type (1949). *An ideal type is one in which the defining attributes are thought to comprise the fundamental essence of the phenomenon in question,* rather than the most common elements noted empirically. Before exploring further what an ideal type is, it is important to understand what it is not. The everyday English word "ideal" connotes something desirable. The term "ideal type" *does not* convey this; an ideal type is not, ipso facto, something desirable or good. An ideal type is not based on the most frequent attributes observed in a variety of real cases, i.e., it is *not* a constructed type.

In creating an ideal type the scholar attempts mentally to understand (mentally construct) what it is about the phenomenon that constitutes its central, defining, essential qualities, in the abstract. Real cases of that phenomenon may rarely if ever exemplify all of the attributes of the ideal type. In other words, the ideal type is an abstraction which one does not expect to find in the real world. Why, then, are ideal types developed? The primary use of types is as a methodological device. Ideal and constructed types serve as yardsticks to use in comparing real cases. For instance, Weber developed an ideal type of bureaucracy (1958a) which lists several attributes he thought comprised the essential qualities of that form of organization. A summary, presented by Etzioni (1964, pp. 53-54), appears in Chart 5.3. One could then study a given organization and, by comparing it with this ideal type, determine the *degree* to which it is bureaucratic. Without such a device, it is often difficult to study, assess, and/or compare complex phenomena. On what basis would you compare several different types of organizations (e.g., a university, the army, Exxon, the March of Dimes)? Your choices are innumerable. The ideal type of bureaucracy gives one list of such bases and, as mentioned above, a base or yardstick to which they may be compared. In short, it might permit you to say that organization X (the army) is more bureaucratic (i.e., closer to the ideal type) than organization Y (your university). One could then search for other variables which might explain why the one organization is more

71

CHART 5.3

SUMMARY OF WEBER'S IDEAL TYPE OF BUREAUCRACY*

1. A continuous organization of official functions bound by *rules*.

2. A specific sphere of competence. This involves *(a)* a sphere of obligations to perform functions which have been marked off as part of a systematic division of labor; *(b)* the provisions of the incumbent with the necessary authority to carry these functions; and *(c)* the necessary means of compulsion are clearly defined and their use is subject to definite conditions.

3. The organization of offices follows the principle of hierarchy; that is, each lower office is under the control and supervision of a higher one.

4. The rules which regulate the conduct of an office may be *technical* rules or norms. In both cases, if their application is to be fully rational, specialized training is necessary. It is thus normally true that only a person who has demonstrated an adequate technical training is qualified to be a member of the administrative staff. . . .

5. It is a matter of principle that the members of the administrative staff should be completely separated from ownership of the means of production or administration. . . . There exists, furthermore, in principle, complete separation of the property belonging to the organization, which is controlled within the spheres of the office, and the personal property of the official. . . .

6. A complete *absence* of appropriation of his official positions by the incumbent is required.

7. Administrative acts, decisions, and rules are formulated and recorded in writing. . . .

8. . . . officials should be compensated by salaries and not receive payments from clients to ensure that their primary orientation be to the organization, to its norms and representatives.

*From Etzioni, 1964, pp. 53-54.

bureaucratic than the other, and in this way develop a theory about bureaucracies.

E. Exemplar

The theory we are developing does not require the use of any classificatory device; the variables are all unidimensional and general. There is, however, one point which can be made about the theory that is relevant to the material discussed in this chapter. The two variables we are attempting to explain, Rate of Labor Force Participation (A) and Occupational Deployment (B), are used in a manner similar to a constructed type. We use the rates of the social majority (white males) on these two dimensions as the yardsticks against which the analogous rates of all other groups are to be compared. White males are thus assumed to constitute the norm, and other groups are assumed to approximate equity with that norm only to the extent that their rates approximate those of white males. If we wished to examine any other society using this theory, we would need first to discover what group constitutes the social (not necessarily numerical) majority and substitute that group for the American category "white males."

STUDENT EXERCISES

1. Develop a taxonomy of families, given two dimensions: (1) division of labor (sex-specific, non-sex-specific); (2) authority structure (equalitarian, matriarchal, patriarchal). Label each of the six resulting types and then define each type.
2. For each of the following multidimensional concepts list at least three unidimensional variables into which it could be broken:
   a. Social class
   b. Masculinity
   c. Suburbia
3. For each of the following create value categories that are mutually exclusive and all-inclusive:
   a. Educational level attained
   b. Type of geographic community (e.g., suburban, small town)
   c. Political preference
   d. Group size
4. Choose one of the following and develop an ideal type:
   a. Democracy
   b. Capitalism
   c. Industrialized society
   Why do you emphasize the traits you have chosen?

CHAPTER **6**

Propositions: The Substance of Theories

If you were to be handed a sociological theory, what you would most probably see would be words (except for a few which would consist of mathematical symbols). In the last two chapters the nature and uses of words were discussed. Some of the words might be organized into assumptions, which form the background for the theory. Others would be organized into definitions, clarifying the meaning of the key concepts and classifications in the theory. Together, the assumptions and definitions would not, however, represent an explanation of anything. Explanation, the *raison d'etre* for all theories, is conveyed through a series of statements called propositions. Propositions constitute the heart and substance of theories. *A proposition is a statement which asserts something about reality by stating relationships between (linking) two or more concepts (variables).* Since they are truth-asserting, propositions are amenable, albeit not directly, to empirical testing. In short, unlike definitions and assumptions, they may be shown to be true or false in a given test. A proposition that has been repeatedly subjected to testing, and just as repeatedly been supported by the data, is known as a *scientific law.* In other words, laws are *propositions which scientists accept as "true."* In sociology few propositions qualify for the title "scientific law." A theory consists of several propositions which,

75

collectively, purport to explain some aspect of reality. Those propositions may or may not have the status of scientific laws.

A. LINKING CONCEPTS

The simplest proposition is a statement linking two concepts. Note that there is no such thing as a proposition relating less than two phenomena which can vary or take on different values (i.e., you cannot use a variable and a constant to form a proposition). An example of a simple proposition might be "the greater the cohesiveness of a group, the greater its efficiency in pursuing group goals." In this case "group cohesiveness" and "efficiency in pursuit of group goals" constitute the two phenomena which can vary. (Presumably, they have already been carefully defined.) Such statements as "In the United States the rate of technological change is constantly increasing" is not a proposition as stated, since there is only one thing that can vary—the rate of technological change. It is thus a possible assertion of fact, but not a theoretical proposition. The same general idea could, however, be restated as a theoretical proposition, such as: "the greater the degree of industrialization, the more rapid the rate of technological change." In this case, the type of society as well as the rate of technological change can vary. Another example of a statement that is not a proposition is "social conflict exists in all societies." There are no variables in this statement as phrased. To say something in propositional form about conflict, one would have to talk about variations in the degree, intensity, or some other attribute of conflict. Societies, too, would have to be treated as a variable according to some attribute. One example might be "the more heterogeneous the society, the more frequent the conflicts within it."

In Chapter 4, logical terms were distinguished from extralogical terms. Unlike the latter, words of the former type are not defined in a given theory. They are, however, crucial in determining the meaning of a proposition. The simplest form of a proposition uses logical words that convey nothing more than mere relationship between concepts (i.e., correlation). The nature of that relationship is left unspecified. The proposition linking group cohesiveness and efficiency in pursuit of group goals is an example: it merely tells us that the two phenomena vary directly (the greater the one, the greater the other). The explanatory nature of the relationship is unclear, since, as discussed in Chapter 2, causality cannot be directly inferred from correlation.

Zetterberg (1965, pp. 69-71) lists five means of specifying more precisely the ways in which the concepts in a proposition are related to one another. A proposition can be stated in such a way that on each of the following dimensions it is clear which of the two alternatives is chosen; (1) reversible-irreversible; (2) deterministic-stochastic; (3) sequential-coextensive; (4) sufficient-contingent; (5) necessary-substitutable.

Reversible-irreversible. A proposition is reversible when it makes sense to add "vice versa" to it, and irreversible if it does not. For example, the proposition "the harder students work, the more they will learn" is irreversible. It is not at all evident that the converse is true: the more students learn the harder they will work. However, the proposition "The more a team practices, the more likely it is to win games" may be reversible; it makes sense to add "vice versa" and assume that winning games will further motivate team members to practice.

Deterministic-stochastic. A proposition is stochastic when the word "probably" or its equivalent is used, and deterministic when the sentence conveys that something will always occur if something else does. As pointed out in Chapter 2, almost all sociological explanations are stochastic. The proposition concerning the extent to which teams practice and win games was stated stochastically through the use of the logical term "more likely." In the form stated above, student work and learning were related deterministically (although in reality that is probably not true).

Sequential-coextensive. A sequential linkage conveys that something must occur prior in time to something else; a coextensive linkage does not assume a time dimension. "The more people were punished physically as youngsters, the more likely they are to punish their own children physically" is an example of a sequential linkage. An example of a coextensive proposition is "the greater the group morale, the more efficiently it performs its tasks"; group morale and task performance occur at the same time.

Sufficient-contingent. A sufficient linkage is one that specifies that if something occurs, something else will also occur, regardless of anything else. Contingent linkages state that the result occurs only if the original input plus something else occur. According to Zetterberg (1965, p. 71) sufficient linkages are rare in sociology. In Chapter 2, the theory presented by Bendix and Lipset (1964) concerning rates of upward social mobility and level of industrialization was discussed as a sufficient explanation. Stated in loose propositional form, that theory would assert that: the achievement of a fairly high level of industrialization is sufficient to bring about a certain (fairly high) rate of intergenerational upward social mobility. More typically, sociologists might make contingent statements such as "all else being equal, the harder a team practices, the more likely it is to win." The "all else being equal" constitutes an open-ended statement of contingency, which might include the available talent, the expertise of the coaches, and so on. An alternative and more informative means of expressing contingency is to state contingencies as specified "givens": "Given equal talent and coaching, the team that practices most will win the most games."

Necessary-substitutable. Again, this distinction parallels one made in Chapter 2 concerning types of explanations. *A necessary linkage is one in which a certain factor must be present to bring about another, while a substitutable linkage states various alternatives which may result in the same thing.* Recalling Lenski's theory (1966) presented in that context, a loosely stated, necessary proposition might be: in order for a system of inequality to develop, a community must produce at a level greater than minimum subsistence for all members (i.e., economic surplus is necessary for stratification). More typical in sociology are substitutable linkages, although the fact that they are substitutable is usually implicit rather than clearly stated.

It should be clear by now that the linkages employed to connect theoretical concepts within propositions are intimately tied to the type of explanation being developed. A functional explanation, as defined in Chapter 2, can now be seen as a proposition or set of propositions which employ reversible, coextensive, substitutable linkages. A full causal explanation involves necessary, sufficient, sequential, deterministic linkages. To convey in a proposition the exact nature of the linkages in all five ways takes considerable care and precision of language; it is no easy task. Let us take the simple proposition stated earlier, "The greater the cohesiveness of a group, the greater its efficiency in pursuing group goals," and attempt to rewrite it so that it will communicate the linkages fully.

Step 1. We will make this proposition reversible: the greater the cohesiveness of a group, the greater its efficiency in pursuing group goals, and *vice versa*. This implies that the efficient pursuit of goals helps to create cohesiveness as well as cohesiveness impacting efficiency.

Step 2. We will make this proposition stochastic: the greater the cohesiveness of a group, the greater the *likelihood* that it will be more efficient in pursuing group goals, and vice versa.

Step 3. We will make it coextensive, since the two variables seem to be mutually interacting (given our decision to make it reversible): the greater the cohesiveness of a group, the greater the likelihood that it is *simultaneously* more efficient in pursuing group goals, and vice versa.

Step 4. We will make it contingent, given the unlikelihood that cohesiveness and efficiency are the only two important factors influencing one another: *all else being equal*, the greater the cohesiveness of a group, the greater the likelihood that it is simultaneously more efficient in pursuing group goals, and vice versa. It should be noted, however, that the phrase "all else being equal" is so vague that, without further specification of what the "all else" consists of, the proposition cannot be proven false. Where negative evidence is found, one could argue that "all else was not equal."

Step 5. We will make the proposition substitutable, on the assumption that other factors could result in greater efficiency and/or cohesiveness: all else being equal, *one of several possible results* of greater group cohesiveness is a greater likelihood that it is simultaneously more efficient in pursuing group goals, and vice versa. The same problem exists with the phrase "one of several possible results" as we found in "all else being equal." If the postulated result is not found, one could say that one of the other, unspecified results occurred. Thus, the proposition is again unfalsifiable.

We now have a more complex sentence which, however, contains the same extralogical terms as it did when it stated nothing more than a simple relationship. The addition of a number of logical words converted this into a proposition stating the relationship between two variables with substantially more explanatory precision. However, in steps 4 and 5 it also served to make the proposition so vague that it is no longer falsifiable. Clearly, more extralogical terms, specifying what else needs to be "equal" and what other "possible results" may occur, are required to complete the task of rendering this proposition both fully testable and precise in specifying the nature of the linkages between the variables. A possible final rendition might read: given similar types of goals and authority structures, greater group cohesiveness enhances the likelihood of greater efficiency in pursuit of group goals or of greater group morale and interpersonal liking, and vice versa.

B. The Logical Status of Variables Within Propositions

The purpose of theories, and hence of their constituent propositions, is to explain something, or more precisely, to explain the presence or absence of or changes in the value of something. *That which is being explained is called a dependent variable. Variables which are used to explain the dependent variable, but which in turn are not explained within the proposition or theory, are termed independent variables.* In any one proposition or theory, the independent variables are taken as "givens," and no explanation is sought to account for their variation. *Intervening variables are any which form a link between the independent variable(s) and the dependent, and without which the former are not related to the latter.* Intervening variables are thus a type of independent variable.

In a given proposition the determination of which of these three statuses a variable holds rests on how it is used logically, not on any property inherent in the variable itself. For instance, in the proposition "the more a student studies, the more she or he is likely to learn," quantity of study is the independent variable and amount of learning the dependent variable. One could also state a proposition which converts that independent into a dependent variable: "the more a student enjoys a subject, the more she or he is likely to study." The dependent variable in this example could, in turn, be converted to an intervening variable: "the more a student enjoys a subject, the more she or he is likely to study and thus the more she or he is likely to learn." Enjoyment and learning are linked in this proposition only indirectly through the mediating influence of quantity of study.

When creating a theory out of a set of propositions, often several individual propositions will not directly relate to the dependent variable. Rather, they will connect various independent and intervening variables which, only later, are finally related to the dependent variable. It is, however, important to keep the logical status of variables separate in one's mind, or the propositions developed will not add up to a clear explanation of something (i.e., the specific dependent variable). It is only too easy to become sidetracked into attempting to explain variables which are, in fact, independent variables in that theory. Since every independent variable could be treated as a dependent variable, the process is potentially endless. Meanwhile, one would have failed in the initial task of explaining the original dependent variable. Thus, when theorizing, the first task is to delineate clearly the dependent variable. Exercising intellectual self-control, the next task is to delineate only those independent and intervening variables necessary to provide, in toto, the desired type of explanation for the specified dependent variable. All other possible propositions are left for another time and exercise. The same basic intellectual approach can also help in everyday debates, which often become sidetracked, as the original issue (dependent variable) is forgotten in the process of arguing over peripheral issues that arise during the course of discussion.

C. Ordering Propositions

A total theory consists of assumptions, definitions of concepts (including classification schemes), and a series of propositions. The sheer quantity of words and sentences involved may make it very difficult for a reader to follow closely the meaning and logic of the theory and, ultimately, devise ways of testing it. Therefore, some way must be found to organize propositions to enhance the usefulness and testability of the theory. The prime rule of theory construction is maximum parsimony. *Parsimony refers to the brevity, conciseness, and succinctness of the formulation.* A theory which is stated in the fewest possible words without sacrificing the meaning of its content is a parsimonious one. More importantly, a theory which employs the smallest number of variables and propositions necessary to explain the dependent variable is a parsimonious one. The most parsimonious means of stating a theory is a series of mathematical equations. When this is not possible, other techniques are available to help in developing a more clear statement of a theory, the logic of which is easily comprehended.

Five techniques are available which render a theory relatively easier to follow intellectually and to convert into testable form than a simple listing of all propositions. They do not all necessarily help in the creation of more parsimonious theory, however. The first two techniques refer to creating inventories of propositions based on either their dependent or independent variables (Zetterberg, 1965, pp. 88-90). In the first case, each proposition is examined to determine its dependent variable. In some cases that will be the final dependent variable in the theory; in others it will be one of the intervening variables of the total theory. Propositions are then grouped, and subsequently presented together, which share the same type of dependent variable. Thus, the skeleton of the entire theory might look like this:

A. Assumptions
B. Concepts and their definitions
C. Propositions
    1. Propositions with dependent variable "A" which represents an intervening variable in the theory.
    2. Propositions with dependent variable "B" which represents an intervening variable in the theory.
    3. Propositions with dependent variable "C" which represents the dependent variable of the total theory.

The second technique employs the same approach, but the basis for the groupings is the independent variable in each proposition. Again, some of these will be independent variables in the total theory while others may have the status of intervening variable in the complete formulation.

The third technique is designed to follow the step-by-step logic of the total theory more closely. The propositions are ordered as chains (Zetterberg, 1965, pp. 90-92). This means that the first proposition(s) begin with the independent variable(s) of the entire theory. Its dependent variable becomes the independent variable in the next proposition (i.e., it is an intervening variable in the total theory). In turn, the new dependent variable becomes the independent one in the next proposition, and so on until the final dependent variable in the theory is also the dependent variable in the proposition. The skeleton of the entire theory might look like this:

A. Assumptions
B. Concepts and Definitions
C. Propositions
    1. I (the independent variable[s] of the theory) is related to A.
    2. A is related to B.
    3. B is related to C.
    4. C is related to D (the dependent variable of the theory).

In this case, A through C are intervening variables within the whole theory.

The fourth technique for ordering the content of a theory relies on the schematic (diagrammatic) representation of the theory. This technique may replace the listing of propositions or it may be used along with some form of list. In Chapter 2, Chart 2.3, the exemplar theory was presented as a schematic diagram, where the concepts were linked by arrows. This is a frequently employed means of presenting a theory, which is typically supplemented by a discussion of what the diagram and its constituent parts mean. There are other ways to represent a theory in a diagram besides that which we employed, but they are too complex for this primer and are used less frequently.

Unlike the first four techniques for ordering propositions, the fifth and final one involves reducing the total number of propositions and thereby helping to increase the parsimony of a theory. This technique involves the creation of what is called *axiomatic theory*. If you ever studied plane geometry you are already familiar with this form of presenting a theory, whether or not you were aware of it. In this form, *the number of propositions is reduced to the minimum number required in order to be able to deduce all other propositions logically. The basic propositions which are stated as the theory are called axioms or postulates. Those which can be deduced from the axioms, using the rules of logic, are called theorems.* The postulates (axioms) are each logically independent; none can be deduced from the others. There are many rules of logic which may be employed in this process, just as there are many rules pertaining to the solution of algebraic equations. However, in this context, it is not possible to present the rules of logical manipulation.

To exemplify the process by which axiomatic theories are developed, a series of simple, hypothetical propositions will be presented and "common sense" logic employed to reduce these to a minimum number of postulates. Assuming that assumptions have been stated and concepts defined:

Proposition 1. The more those who socialize children employ rewards rather than punishments, the more children will tend to imitate their socializers.

Proposition 2. The more those who socialize children employ rewards rather than punishments, the more secure the children will tend to feel.

Proposition 3. The more children imitate their socializers, the more independence they will tend to be given.

Proposition 4. The more security children feel, the more independence they will tend to be given.

Proposition 5. The more independence children are given, the less they tend to conform to peer pressure.

Proposition 6. The more secure children feel, the less they tend to conform to peer pressures.

There are five variables in these six propositions: the use of rewards rather than punishments (R); the degree to which children imitate their socializers (I); the degree to which children feel secure (S); the degree of independence given children (X); and the extent of conformity to peer pressure (C). Schematically, these six propositions look like this, when ↑ signifies the term "the more" or "the greater," ↓ signifies "the less," and → conveys linkage:

1. ↑ R → ↑ I
2. ↑ R → ↑ S
3. ↑ I → ↑ X
4. ↑ S → ↑ X
5. ↑ X → ↓ C
6. ↑ S → ↓ C

Examining these carefully, we see that if S and I are both related to R (propositions 1 and 2), they must be related to each other (a proposition which is not stated and is thus a theorem). Therefore, if I is related to X (proposition 3), then S must also be related to X, since it is related to I. Thus, proposition 4 can be deduced and need not be stated initially. We can also see that if R is related to S and I (propositions 1 and 2), and in turn I is related to X (proposition 3), then R must also be related to X (a proposition which is not stated and is thus also a theorem). Given these relationships (i.e., between R, on the one hand, and X and S on the other), it is possible to replace propositions 4 and 5 with one new one: ↑R → ↓C. From this one new proposition, one could work backwards to deduce the relationship between C, on the one hand, and X, S, or I on the other. Our axiomatic theory would now contain four postulates:

84

1 ↑ R → ↑ I
2. ↑ R → ↑ S
3. ↑ I → ↑ X
4. ↑ R → ↓ C

We could then deduce the following by exhausting the logically possible combinations of the five variables (i.e., these six plus the four axioms connect each variable with the remaining four):

1. ↑ R → ↑ X
2. ↑ I → ↑ S
3. ↑ I → ↓ C
4. ↑ X → ↑ S
5. ↑ X → ↓ C
6. ↑ S → ↓ C

Note that we began this exercise with six propositions. We end with a more parsimonious theory consisting of only four postulates. Moreover, we can derive six theorems from these, resulting in ten rather than six propositions. The scientist has been given a total of four new insights in the process of this exercise in logic.

The purpose of rendering a theory in axiomatic form is twofold: parsimony and the creation of new insights. The example given above shows how, by applying logical principles, new sociological understanding may be generated. This is clearly a very important function for any theory to provide.

D. EXEMPLAR

The time has come to discuss the meaning of the chart summarizing our theory, presented in Chapter 2 (Chart 2.3). In this theory there are two final dependent variables, Rate of Labor Force Participation (A) and Occupational Deployment Patterns (B), which are linked to one another. The four variables collected together as C represent the main independent variables in the theory. Other variables, such as G, are not related in any way to C and should thus also be considered as independent variables. The remainder are, minimally, indirectly linked to C and are thus intervening variables. Each arrow connecting two variables could be stated as a proposition. This would result in twenty-seven propositions—clearly beyond the scope of this exercise to develop. It is, however, possible to reduce this number somewhat by using more than two variables in some of the propositions. In what follows, two- and three-variable propositions are developed to account for the relationships which are most important in the theory. However, since the purpose of doing this is to exemplify the material presented in this chapter, not to explicate the details of this particular theory, no attempt to cover the entire theory and all possible linkages will be made.

Proposition 1. The demand for labor (dependent variable) tends to vary in response to a complex interplay (conjuncture) of the variables of level of technology, state of the economy, availability of natural resources, and population size (independent variables), among other, more minor influences. The linkages in this proposition are irreversible, stochastic, sequential, contingent, and implicitly substitutable. It is the only proposition in the entire theory to employ those variables considered as the main independent variables of the theory. Using the same letters to designate each variable that were used in Chart 2.3, this proposition can be presented as: C → D.

Proposition 2. Holding constant the extent to which alternative occupations are available to group members (intervening variable), the more members of the group which usually fills an occupational role pursue vocational training (independent variable), the greater will be the supply of traditional labor force participants (dependent variable). The linkages in this proposition are irreversible, deterministic, sequential, contingent, and implicitly substitutable. K, ↑ H → ↑ E

Proposition 3. The more the members of a group which usually fills an occupational role define that work as important and desirable (independent variable), the greater the supply of traditional labor force participants tends to be (dependent variable). The linkages in this proposition are irreversible, stochastic, coextensive, implicitly contingent, and implicitly substitutable. ↑ J → ↑ E

Proposition 4. Holding constant the extent to which alternative occupations are available to group members (intervening variable), the more positive the definitions and evaluations of the capabilities of members of the group which usually fills an occupational role (independent variable), the greater the supply of traditional labor force participants (dependent variable) tends to be. The linkages are irreversible, stochastic, coextensive, contingent, and implicitly substitutable. K, ↑ I → ↑ E

Proposition 5. The greater the social movement activity on behalf of a social minority group (independent variable), the more positive the definitions and evaluations of actor capabilities of group members (dependent variable) will tend to become. The linkages are irreversible, stochastic, sequential, implicitly contingent, and implicitly substitutable. $\uparrow L \rightarrow \uparrow I$

Proposition 6. The greater the social movement activity on behalf of a social minority group (independent variable) the greater the probability that political and legal policies will change in that group's favor (dependent variable). The linkages are irreversible, stochastic, sequential, implicitly contingent, and implicitly substitutable. $\uparrow L \rightarrow \uparrow M$

Proposition 7. Holding constant the supply of traditional labor force participants (intervening variable), the greater the demand for labor (independent variable), the greater the demand for nontraditional labor force participants (dependent variable). The linkages are irreversible, deterministic, coextensive, contingent, and implicitly substitutable. $E, \uparrow D \rightarrow \uparrow F$. Indeed, given our definition of F (see Chapter 4), this proposition is true by definition and is thus tautological to state as a proposition.

Proposition 8. Holding constant the demand for labor (intervening variable), the smaller the supply of traditional labor force participants (independent variable), the greater the demand for nontraditional labor force participants (dependent variable). The linkages are irreversible, deterministic, coextensive, contingent, and implicitly substitutable. $D, \downarrow E \rightarrow \uparrow F$. The same problem of tautology exists here as in Proposition 7.

Proposition 9. The greater the demand for nontraditional labor force participants (independent variable), the greater the rate of labor force participation among social minorities (dependent variable). The linkages are irreversible, deterministic, coextensive, implicitly contingent, and implicitly substitutable. $\uparrow F \rightarrow \uparrow A$

Proposition 10. The more positive the definitions and evaluations of the capabilities of minority group members, the greater their rate of labor force participation and the more similar to the social majority group their pattern of occupational deployment tends to be, and vice versa. As a reversible proposition, it does not make sense to label the variables as independent or dependent; each is simultaneously both. In addition to reversible, the linkages are stochastic, coextensive, implicitly contingent, and implicitly substitutable. $\uparrow I \leftrightarrow \uparrow A, \uparrow B$

Proposition 11. The greater the social movement activity on behalf of a social minority group, the greater its rate of labor force participation and the more similar to the social majority its occupational deployment pattern tends to be, and vice versa. Again, this linkage is reversible, and, therefore, one cannot delineate the logical status of the variables. In addition, the linkages are stochastic, coextensive, implicitly contingent, and implicitly substitutable. ↑ L ←→ ↑ A, ↑ B

Proposition 12. The more political and legal policy is changed to benefit a social minority (independent variable), the higher its rate of labor force participation and the more similar to the social majority its occupational deployment pattern (dependent variables) will tend to become. The linkages are irreversible, stochastic, sequential, implicitly contingent, and implicitly substitutable. ↑ M → ↑ A, ↑ B

Summarizing these twelve propositions using the letter symbols presented in Chart 2.3 and above:

```
 1.    C  →  D
 2.    K, ↑  H  → ↑ E
 3.  ↑ J  → ↑ E
 4.    K, ↑  I  → ↑ E
 5.  ↑ L  → ↑ I
 6.  ↑ L  → ↑ M
 7.    E, ↑  D  → ↑ F
 8.    D, ↑  E  → ↑ F
 9.  ↑ F  → ↑ A
10.  ↑ I ←→ ↑ A, ↑  B
11.  ↑ L ←→ ↑ A, ↑  B
12.  ↑ M  → ↑ A, ↑  B
```

This is scarcely a highly parsimonious, axiomatic theory at this stage of its development. The propositions are presented more or less as a chain, beginning with the theory's main independent variables and ending with its dependent variables. However, given the systemic nature of the theory, which means that many, if not most of the variables are interconnected with one another, it is impossible to present sequentially a series of propositions as a simple chain. That is one important reason for presenting this type of theory in diagrammatic form; the interrelations are made clearly evident.

Despite the fact that the theory is not presented axiomatically, several further relationships can be deduced from the twelve propositions presented. For instance, given that H, J, and I all vary directly with E (Propositions 2-4), one can infer that H, J, and I vary directly with one another. Indeed, an examination of the chart shows arrows connecting each with the remaining two. A relationship not pictured in Chart 2.3 can also be inferred: since L is related to I and M in the same way (Propositions 5 and 6), one could infer a relationship between I and M. Similarly, I, L, and M are all related directly to A and B, thus implying relationships between I, L, and M. Two of these (L to M and L to I) appear on the chart; the third (M to I) does not. Many other such exercises could be done with the result that almost all of the linkages noted on the chart, plus others not depicted, could probably be derived. Thus, new insights arise despite the fact that this is not a fully axiomatic theory.

The actual theory consists of the chart presented in Chapter 2, the assumptions discussed in Chapter 3, the concepts as defined primarily in Chapter 4, and the propositions enumerated in this chapter. In presenting such a theory, the author(s) would also typically discuss the general meaning and importance of their approach. This discussion may be viewed as the "flesh" which fills out the "skeleton," i.e., the actual elements of the theory as listed above.

Briefly, the theory presented in the Exemplar attempts to explain the conditions under which various social minorities (gender, racial, and/or ethnic) are more (or less) similar to a social majority (e.g., white males in the United States) in terms of rates of labor force participation and patterns of occupational deployment. The theory suggests that the primary impetus for change in the two dependent variables is the extent of demand for non-traditonal labor. This variable changes in response to two others: the supply of traditional labor force participants and the general demand for workers. A series of mostly economic variables affect the general demand for workers. The supply of traditional workers for a given occupation is affected by some social psychological variables, the acquisition of necessary training by such people, and the presence or absence of alternative occupational roles. As minority groups become more similar in labor force participation and deployment patterns to the social majority, they tend to create social movements. In turn, movements further affect their labor force participation rates and occupational deployment patterns, as well as some of the relevant social psychological variables and legal-political policies. Such changes tend to be fought by traditional labor force groups. To the extent that a movement is successful in changing legal and political policies and the specified social psychological variables, they, too, tend to change the dependent variables further. The theory is presented as reversible, i.e., a social minority can be pushed out of the labor force and/or out of certain occupations, and, therefore, become more dissimilar to the social majority. The same variables presumably are involved irrespective of the direction of change (toward greater similarity or dissimilarity). The major differences between this theory and many other approaches to explaining the same dependent variables is our emphasis on demand factors—the socioeconomic factors which pull minority group members into (or push them out of) the labor force and cause changes in deployment patterns. Other theories often emphasize attributes of minority groups which affect the members' availability for employment generally or for particular occupations, namely, supply factors.

STUDENT EXERCISES

1. For each of the following pairs of variables write a clear and complete proposition. Specify the nature of the linkages within each on all five dimensions. Justify the linkages you specify. Which is the dependent and which the independent variable in each?
   a. Loudness of music; popularity of rock group
   b. Income; rate of "soft" drug (cocaine, marajuana) use
   c. Cultural relativism; formal education; extent of foreign travel
   d. Degree of centralized decision making; degree of efficiency
   e. Intelligence; interest in school; age
2. Following are five variables. Select one which will serve as the dependent variable for your theory. Write as many propositions as you need, using the other four, to explain your dependent variable. Each variable must be used at least once. Place your propositions into a meaningful order and explain what that order is. Using logic, can you reduce the number of propositions without sacrifice of meaning? Do so if you are able.
   a. Degree of conformity to organizational norms
   b. Extent of upward mobility within the organization
   c. Degree of creativity
   d. Degree of popularity
   e. Hours worked overtime
3. In Chapter 1, Exercise 5, you either read a theory or you developed a tentative explanation yourself. Now, take that theory or explanation and put it into propositional form, that is, specify the variables and do the same steps as in Number 2 above.

90

CHAPTER 7

Testing and Revising Theories

Throughout this primer, stress has been placed on the necessary relationship between theory and research. In formulating theories, attention must be paid to how they can be empirically tested. In doing research, one is often guided by one or more theoretical formulations. This primer is not designed to instruct the reader in specific research techniques. However, there are a number of general methodological issues involved in testing theories which need to be included in this discussion. Many of these issues also pertain to sociological research conducted for purposes other than the testing of theories.

The process of testing and revising a theory requires a series of steps. Scientists do not necessarily follow these stages in precise sequence. In fact, they cannot accomplish the early stages without knowing, with some degree of surety, what they will do during the latter ones. However, each of the following must be accomplished in the process of theory testing and revision:

1. Formulating the research problem, that is, converting an abstract theory into a series of clearly stated, researchable questions.

2. Developing a research design by creating a general scheme or plan for finding the information necessary to answer the questions posed in Number 1.

3. Developing a sampling design—deciding on the units to be studied.

4. Developing and administering the research instrument, that is,

operationalizing variables and actually accumulating the facts necessary to answer the questions posed in Number 1.

5. Analyzing the results, seeing to what extent the facts accumulated in Number 4 support the theory.

6. Revising the theory (if necessary) by changing parts of it in order to account better for the observed facts.

A. The Research Problem

Theories consist of assumptions, concepts (including classifications) and their definitions, and a series of propositions. The assumptions are not, by their very nature, subject to empirical test. The concepts, if defined properly, do not assert anything about reality and are, therefore, not testable. That means that testing a theory must involve testing the relationships specified in the propositions.

Theoretical propositions employ concepts that are relatively high in level of abstraction. These concepts represent variable phenomena and must be stated in more concrete, less abstract form in order to be tested. In this form the concepts become "variables." Thus, for instance, the concept "deviance" may be converted into the variable "rates of specified crimes" (burglary, assault, rape, theft, etc.) or into a large number of other variables which refer to noncriminal types of deviance. *A proposition which relates two or more variables together* (rather than two or more theoretical concepts) *is called an hypothesis.* When one conducts research, one tests hypotheses. Thus, the first issue concerns how one goes about converting propositions into hypotheses.

The conversion problem in essence involves the development of a research instrument. This is one manifestation of the need to consider later stages during the early steps of the testing process. The conversion occurs when a variable replaces a concept in a proposition. The chief concern is that of validity: is each variable a valid indicator of the relevant concept (see Chapter 4)? There are usually innumerable variables which can validly reflect any one concept. Therefore, any one proposition can be rendered into a vast number of different hypotheses. Take, for instance, the simple proposition "the greater the cohesiveness of a group, the greater its efficiency in pursuing group goals." "Group cohesiveness" is a relatively abstract concept. The following variables, among others, might validly reflect it:

1. Interpersonal communication among group members

92

2. A shared feeling of "we-ness" (group belonging)

3. Cooperation (mutual help) in performing tasks

4. Shared norms unique to the group

The concept "efficiency" also provides alternative possibilities, such as:

1. Units of output per total group

2. Units of output per person

3. Reduction of wasted materials

Using only these seven (total) variables, there are twelve possible simple hypotheses (although many others of a more complex nature could also be developed using three or more variables in each). A few of these twelve are:

1. The more interpersonal communication there is among group members, the greater the number of units of output per person.

2. The more cooperation in task performance among group members, the greater the number of units of output per group.

3. The more group members share a feeling of "we-ness," the greater the reduction of wasted materials.

Since a theory consists of a number of propositions, each proposition can be rendered into a large variety of different hypotheses, and each hypothesis can be tested in a large variety of settings, one could spend forever testing one theory. One way to shorten the task is to test the same hypotheses in radically different situations. If the data support the hypotheses in a few extremely varied situations, one may have more faith in them than if they were supported in a larger number of tests in very similar situations. For example, if the three hypotheses presented above were tested in a large corporation, the army, a university, and a hospital, it would be better than twenty tests all conducted in corporations. This is basically an issue of sampling which would have to be considered in this early stage of developing the research problem. Similarly, the use of the most widely differing variables to represent the same concept usually gives more information for less work than the use of highly similar ones. In the example above, "reduction of wasted materials" is very different from "units of output per total group" or "per person." The latter two are, however, quite similar. Testing hypotheses using the first and either the second or third would probably be about as fruitful as testing three hypotheses, one each for each variable. These decisions are linked to the creation of a research instrument.

Typically, when a theory is developed at least some of the propositions will have been previously tested, that is, data probably exist which gave the theorist the initial insight upon which to develop the propositions. It is, therefore, a better use of scarce time and resources to test those for which there is little or no existing evidence. However, where time and resources permit, replication of past research is always advisable to provide added support (or possibly disconfirmation) for the theory. Ultimately, replication of the research of others is always necessary if we are to have faith in research findings and the generalizations based on those findings.

In the last chapter, the logical connection between propositions was discussed. If the theory is presented in axiomatic form (or even in a quasi-axiomatic way), one can test hypotheses derived from postulates *or* selected theorems and, employing logic, make assumptions about the remaining propositions based on the research findings. In short, one picks those logically most central propositions (which have not been previously tested) to convert into testable hypotheses (Zetterberg, 1965, Chapter 8).

Some propositions are inherently more difficult to test than others or may be impossible to test in the research settings available. Again, using logic, one can derive alternative ones (presumably easier to test) from which the original one can be deduced (Zetterberg, 1965, pp. 163-164). There is no loss in not subjecting the original proposition to a test, since it is in fact tested by indirect inference.

A rough test of a theory is to make one general hypothesis and test for it. If two or more competing theories lead to logically contradictory propositions about the same phenomenon, this is one approach to evaluating which is better. If, for instance, one theory resulted in the hypothesis that revolutions occur during periods of economic depression and another that they occurred as economic conditions began to improve, one could examine a series of revolutions and the economic conditions prevalent in those societies immediately before the upheavals occurred. The data should allow us to determine which (if either) is more correct. As Zetterberg (1965, pp. 166-167) points out, however, one can be right for the wrong reasons. The two theories in question would probably each involve an explanation of why a given economic condition leads to revolution. One of the postulated relationships between economic conditions and revolution may be correct, but the reason adduced could be wrong. Without a test of other propositions in that theory one cannot know if the explanation (i.e., the bulk of the theory) was supported or not. What we have, in effect, is simply a correlational statement, and you should recall from Chapter 2 that correlation and explanation are not one and the same thing.

Taking all these considerations into account, a number of propositions is selected and converted into a manageable number of hypotheses. The number finally selected is always constrained by time and resources available to conduct the research. Together, the final group of hypotheses constitute the research problem.

B. The Research Process

In this section, some basic issues pertaining to research design, sampling, and the development and administration of the research instrument will be discussed.

A research design is a general strategy or master plan for conducting a piece of research. The design should be carefully articulated with the research problem if the research findings are going to be capable of providing the types of answers relevant to the questions raised. However, there are often practical and/or ethical reasons why a research design is not perfectly articulated with the research problem. There are many types of research designs. The following are brief discussions of a few of the basic types, the conditions under which they are most appropriately used, and some of the problems involved in their use.

Experimental design. The single best method to test a causal proposition is to use an experimental design. In this design *the researcher structures a situation such that the hypothesized causal (independent) variable is the only (known) relevant input into a situation.* Any noted change in the dependent variable can then be said, with substantial confidence, to result from the independent variable. This is usually done in a laboratory setting where all possible stimuli except for the independent variable are carefully controlled. Typically, in the classic experimental design, subjects are divided into two categories, the control group and the experimental group (although often there are several experimental groups). They are both given a "before test." The control group experiences nothing else. The experimental group(s) is administered the "stimulus" (i.e., the independent variable). An "after test" is then given to both groups to determine if the supposed causal variable has had the hypothesized effect. For instance, we might test the hypothesis that "seeing a film about natural childbirth causes a reduction in fear among pregnant women." Two groups of pregnant women could be asked about their feelings concerning childbirth and pain. The experimental group could then be shown a film about natural childbirth. Both groups would then be requestioned. Greater changes in the expressed feelings of the experimental compared to the control group would be evidence in support of the hypothesis, since no other variables except viewing or not viewing the film intervened to differentiate the two groups. This design could be made more elaborate, for instance, by establishing another experimental group which received a lecture instead of the film, and in this way the relative effectiveness of two approaches could be assessed.

There are a number of complicated variations of experimental design. There are also types of quasi-experimental designs which approach these conditions but do not totally fulfill them. Regardless of whether the design is fully or partially experimental, there are problems involved in employing this approach. Unfortunately, many propositions developed by sociologists are not amenable to conversion into a laboratory setting. Also, people may react differently in the contrived setting of a laboratory than in "natural settings," and, therefore, the knowledge gained from experiments may not be transferable to other contexts. Finally, many potential experiments cannot be done because of ethical considerations which can arise when one manipulates human beings.

Panel design. Another design which is appropriate for testing causal propositions *involves gathering data from the same people over a period of time.* Recall that to infer cause-and-effect relationships, one must demonstrate that the independent variable precedes the dependent in time. This design would be useful if, for instance, one wished to test the hypothesis "compared to being child-free, having children tends to cause an increase in marital strain." One would develop a measure of marital strain and repeatedly administer it to the same couples (the "panel"), beginning at the time of marriage and ending many years later (after many of the couples had had children). This is superior to a simple comparison of child-free couples and those with children, since the latter group could have been characterized by more marital strain than the former even before they had children. The panel design allows one to trace changes, not merely examine differences between groups. It is not as good as an experimental design for inferring causal relationships because no direct control can be exercised over other variables which may impact the dependent variable. Panel designs are relatively rare in sociology for practical reasons. Each time the researcher tries to recontact the members of the panel, he or she will find that many have moved and cannot be located, have died, or have tired of participating. The panel usually grows smaller with each successive wave of the study. Moreover, this is a very expensive type of research, since every effort must be made to locate as many of the original subjects as possible. Finally, it entails substantial patience, since a decade or more may have to pass before the project is completed.

A variant of this design is the *longitudinal design which retests over time, but the people tested each time are different.* This reduces many of the problems of the panel design, but is much weaker for inferring causal relationships. It might be used, for instance, in a case where one wished to test the hypothesis "the closer an election comes in time, the more people discuss politics with their friends." However, if one found that those questioned two days before an election discuss politics more than those questioned two months earlier, it could not be assumed that the hypothesized changes occurred. It could be the case that the latter group was simply more interested in politics than the former and had been discussing it just as much months earlier.

Cross-sectional design. This design is both the weakest for testing causal statements and the most frequently used in sociology. In this design *people are studied at only one point in time and various subgroups within the total sample are compared to one another, or the relationships between different variables as they are distributed within the samples are examined.* The hypothesis discussed earlier concerning having children and marital strain could be tested using a cross-sectional design. A number of married people, with and without children, would be tested for degree of marital strain. The two groups, those with children and the child-free, would then be compared to see if, indeed, the former are characterized by more strain than the latter. The problem, as mentioned earlier, is that those with children may have had more strain all along, and this cannot be known from a cross-sectional approach. Thus, one cannot be sure that having children causes an increase in marital strain. The relationship found is a correlation only, and again, correlation does not demonstrate causality. However, this design is entirely appropriate to test propositions and theories which do not imply a time dimension, for example, for functional explanations and propositions with coextensive linkages.

Why is the cross-sectional design so popular among sociologists even when causal statements are being tested? For essentially practical reasons: it is quicker and relatively cheaper than panel or longitudinal designs. Many of the social-science-based findings and conclusions presented by the media of mass communication are based on cross-sectional studies. You should, therefore, exercise some skepticism before accepting those conclusions if they imply causality. The various public opinion polls that are conducted, especially around election time, are often longitudinal in design. One can place more faith in them because of this, but the shortcomings of that design should be recalled when evaluating the information presented.

To test a theory, a researcher selects a research design that maximizes her or his ability to draw inferences which articulate well with the type of explanation embodied in the theory. However, it is clear that available time and resources, and sometimes ethical considerations, may force the researcher to settle for a design which is less than ideal for testing a specific theory.

The next stage in the process of testing a theory involves choosing the actual units to be studied. *A population consists of all cases which fit a set of specifications.* If one developed a theory (or its relevant hypotheses) which pertains to bureaucratic organizations in general, then all such organizations in existence form the relevant population. Likewise, if the theory (or hypotheses) pertains to people in industrialized nations, then all such people constitute the relevant population. Looked at from a different perspective, the population is the category of people or units to which the findings of a given study can be generalized.

A sample is that part of a population actually studied in a given research project. Occasionally a researcher studies an entire population, especially if it is very small, or data, such as those provided by the United States Census Bureau, are already available. Most of the time, however, there is no reason to spend the amount of resources necessary to study an entire population. A well-drawn sample, even though it only represents a minute proportion of the population, can give the researcher a highly accurate picture of the population. A "well-drawn" sample is one which is representative of the population, that is, is without systematic bias. Systematic biasing of a sample means that parts of the population fail to be represented in the sample or are underrepresented while other parts are overrepresented.

There are a number of different sampling designs that can be employed, but a discussion of them is not directly relevant to this primer. The important points to understand in this context are twofold. First, adequate test of a theory ultimately involves the definition of a population (and hence sample) which reflects the scope of that theory. A theory about bureaucracies is not adequately tested when only governmental or only corporate bureaucracies are examined. A given research project may define the population as only one type. The findings, however, could only be generalized to that type, and the project thus represents a very limited test of the theory. Eventually, the entire population of bureaucracies (i.e., all types of bureaucratic organizations) must be sampled if one is to test the general theory adequately.

The second important point is that, in the absence of a representative sample, reliable conclusions about the population cannot be drawn. Simply put, those components systematically omitted from the sample may not behave in the same way as those included. Imagine the situation where the population is defined as all students at your school. The sample is drawn by someone standing in the foyer of the library. The type of students who frequent the library (and are thus available for the sample) are probably very different in a variety of ways from those who do not. The bias thus built into the sample would make it impossible to say anything accurate about all students at your school. Theory testing requires faith in the sample as representative of the population. If the sample is improperly drawn, the population for which the theory is being tested may not be known, and thus the results of the test may be hard to interpret in terms of the theory.

One way to insure that the sample is representative of the population is to employ some variety (and there are several) of random sampling. *Random sampling means that every unit in the population has an equal chance of being selected into the sample.* Selecting a random sample is based on theories of probability; this is not to be confused with accidental or haphazard sampling of available units. In the example above, students who do not use the library cannot be selected; those who do may be. Thus, all students do not have an equal chance of being in the sample, and the sample is not random but is haphazard or accidental. Nonrandom sampling is often easier and sometimes less expensive to do than random. Indeed, it is impossible to sample randomly some populations (e.g., those engaged in deviant acts that they attempt to hide from others). Nonrandom sampling can give a researcher many insights which may provide the starting point in developing a theory. However, nonrandom sampling should not be used for theory testing if it can be avoided.

The next step in the testing process is to determine what data will actually be collected from the units in the sample, and what technique(s) will be used to collect them. The hypotheses which constitute the research problem contain the variables for which data are sought. In other words, each variable is given an operational definition which specifies the type of information sought. Take, for example, a proposition which includes the concept "intelligence." The concept may be converted into the operationalized variable "score on a standard IQ test." Thus, the sample members will each be asked to complete that test. *The sum total of all the operationalizations constitute the research instrument* for a given research project. This determines the data actually collected.

In actual fact, more data are routinely collected than pertain merely to those variables which constitute the hypotheses being tested. This occurs for two reasons. First, the basic costs, in terms of time and money, involved in collecting data are high, but the addition of some extra variables adds little to those basic costs. Since the same data can serve many purposes, within reason, it makes practical sense to collect more than are needed for the original purpose. However, there is a limit to how long an instrument can get before the subjects develop fatigue or refuse to participate. Second, to the extent that any of the original hypotheses are not supported, the additional data may enable the researcher to test alternative or revised hypotheses without having to conduct a totally new research project. Determining what variables to add, over and above those in the original hypotheses, requires making educated guesses concerning alternative formulations of the original hypotheses and/or about other possible uses of the data. Most researchers have experienced that frustrated feeling when, in the latter stages of the process, they say "if only I had gathered some information about . . ."

There is a large array of specific techniques involved in designing and administering a research instrument. Again, it is beyond the scope of this primer to discuss these in any detail. However, a few points are relevant in this context. Excluding the use of already existing data (which still had to be collected by someone, somehow), there are only two basic ways to collect sociologically relevant information: ask people to answer questions and/or observe human behavior or the products of that behavior. The two are not mutually exclusive, and both may be done in one research project. Which one is chosen or emphasized is dependent upon how the variable is operationalized, which, in turn, is related to the nature of the theoretical concept. Let us take each method in turn and look a bit more closely at it.

A very frequently used technique in theory testing involves asking a sample of people a series of questions about their attitudes, beliefs, values, behaviors, and personal characteristics (e.g., age, income, occupation, sex, race, or ethnicity). The questions asked comprise the operationalized variables. They may be asked verbally in a face-to-face or phone interview and the answer recorded by tape or writing. Alternatively, a self-administered questionnaire can be given to sample members in person or by mail. The questions can include possible answers (structured or closed questions) or require "essay-type" answers (unstructured or open-ended questions).

It is important to note that the way questions are posed and, in the case of structured questions, the answers provided strongly influence the responses. Different wording of the same question and/or answers may yield entirely different results (and therefore lead to different conclusions based on those results). Given the same wording in the question, an open-ended response allows the respondent to relate his or her own perceptions. In responding to a closed question subjects can only choose the answer which represents the closest approximation to their thoughts. Thus, one often gains more in-depth, detailed, and presumably more accurate information using unstructured questions. However, analyzing the responses to open-ended questions is much more difficult than structured questions. Moreover, in the final analysis the researcher must often ignore much of the detail and uniqueness of unstructured answers in order to generalize from the data, thus losing the advantages of this approach.

Regardless of the technique used to question people, the type of information received is *not* how people actually behave. If a theory pertains to actual behavior (rather than attitudes or values, for instance), questioning people is not an adequate means to test it. Reported behavior may provide some information *vis-à-vis* the theory, but people's reports of their behavior may or may not be a very accurate depiction of real behavior. This approach is widely used, however, because a relatively large amount of data can be collected for less money and in far less time than it would take to collect the same amount of data by observation. Moreover, it is often easier to write questions than to develop a systematic means of collecting data through observation.

The behavior of people may be observed by someone participating in the group (participant observer) or by someone who watches without involvement. In either case, there is a major problem in designing a means (research instrument) to ensure that the constant flow of observed behavior can be precisely and systematically recorded in terms of discrete variables. Imagine, for a moment, sitting in a room with a group of six interacting people and trying to measure carefully "the degree of interpersonal interaction." Ironically, then, while a hypothesis concerning actual human behavior should be tested by observing that behavior, it is often difficult to observe it with sufficient precision to test the hypothesis adequately. Furthermore, the very fact that the group is being observed has some influence on its members' behavior, and thus the findings may not be an accurate reflection of a more "natural" situation. Finally, a lot of time is involved in observing one group, and, as discussed earlier, adequate theory testing requires data from many settings. For these reasons observational studies are most often used to generate insights upon which theories may be developed, rather than to test existing theories. Alternatively, observation is used in combination with some form of questioning. If the results of both imperfect approaches are similar, more faith can be placed in the hypothesis than if only one technique is employed.

The final type of study involves "observing" the products of human behavior. This approach minimizes the danger of subjects reacting to being studied, or behaving differently because of the research experience. In this type of study, subjects do not know they are being studied. If one had a hypothesis that "the wealthy consume more hard liquor than the poor," one could rummage through a random sample of garbage pails in wealthy and poor neighborhoods, searching for empty bottles (see Webb, *et al.*, 1966). In the example used earlier in this chapter, output per group or person could be measured by looking at output records kept by the organization. Media of communication can be studied as reflections of cultural norms through a procedure called content analysis, which is a systematic way of "observing" the content of books, movies, newspapers, and so on. The chief problem with observing the products of human behavior is that much of the time those necessary to test a given hypothesis do not exist and/or are unavailable to the researcher. Again, the chief use of this approach is combining it with another method.

It should be clear by now that each stage involved in the process of designing research and collecting data should be as carefully related to the particular theory being tested as is possible in practical and ethical terms. Since practical considerations normally prevent an ideal test of a theory, repeated tests must be done, often employing different approaches. As more and more evidence accumulates which is consistent, even though each time the procedure was imperfect, one comes to place more and more faith in the theory or hypothesis. However, by now it should be abundantly clear why one never says with surety that a given proposition, theory, or hypothesis is "true."

C. What the Data Can (and Cannot) Tell Us About the Theory

The data are all collected. The issue for this section is: what does one do with them, and how does one reach conclusions about the theory on the basis of the findings?

The hypotheses which comprise the research problem each suggest a particular relationship between two or more variables (e.g., that variable X should increase as variable Y does; that group 1 should be more likely to do something than group 2). *Data analysis generally involves the use of a variety of types of statistics to aid in deciding whether and to what extent the facts (data) support the hypotheses* and hence, by inference, the propositions and theory, *being tested.* There are three general categories of statistics which are relevant to data analysis.

Descriptive statistics are those which *tell us something about the characteristics of the sample or a part of the sample (a subsample).* They include measures of central tendency (the three types of averages: mean, median, and mode), measures of dispersion or spread (e.g., frequency distributions or the percentage and/or number of the sample units which fall into each value category for a given variable), and measures of form (e.g., skewness of a curve). If one knows something about the characteristics of the population, descriptive statistics can help one to determine the degree to which the sample is representative of the population. They may also suggest relationships between variables. For instance, the averages or frequency distributions of two or more subsamples may be compared on some one or more variables. If a hypothesis suggests that two subsamples ought to be different in terms of some variable, the first task might be to examine the descriptive statistics concerning that variable for each of the two groups. If there is no difference, one has disconfirmed the hypothesis as stated, and, therefore, produced evidence adverse to the theory. If there is a difference, one must go on to the next type of statistic.

Tests of significance (e.g., t tests, chi square tests) *tell us the probability of a relationship such as that which appears to exist between variables, (or an apparent difference between groups) occurring by chance.* Samples are never absolutely perfect mirrors of a total population. There is always some probability that the relationships observed within any sample do not reflect reality but rather are the result of chance sampling error. For instance, suppose we sampled several groups and, using descriptive statistics, found that the subsample characterized by "high feelings of we-ness" had a somewhat higher average output per person than the subsample characterized by "low feelings of we-ness." A test of significance would allow us to determine the probability that this finding is not an artifact of our particular sample, that the difference noted is likely to exist within the population.

In statistics the actual research hypothesis is not tested (unless, as sometimes happens, the research hypothesis postulates no relationship). Instead, one tests the *null hypothesis,* namely, *a statement that no difference (no relationship) exists.* In the example above, the null hypothesis would be that "there is no difference in output per person when comparing groups with high feelings of we-ness to groups with low feelings of we-ness." There are two types of errors that can be made in determining whether or not the data support a hypothesis. *Type I is the error of rejecting a true null hypothesis.* Stated in terms of the research, rather than the null hypothesis, this error occurs when you accept as true a false research hypothesis. *Type II is the error of failing to reject a false null hypothesis,* that is, rejecting a true research hypothesis. The probabilities of these two types of errors generally vary inversely: the more likely that a Type I error is being committed, the less likely it is that a Type II error is being committed, and vice versa. In any science, it is more important to guard against accepting as true something which is in fact false (Type I error) than accidentally rejecting a true statement as false (i.e., committing a Type II error). That is, the burden of proof is on the scientist to establish with very considerable surety the veracity of her or his assertions, even if it means rejecting as undemonstrated some things which are in fact true. Our legal system is built on the same principle: guilt must be established beyond doubt. The reasoning is that it is better to let a guilty person go free than to punish someone who is innocent. For this reason, the standards for preventing Type I error are very high, thereby increasing the likelihood of Type II error. By convention, for a test of significance to demonstrate satisfactorily that a noted difference is not an artifact of the sample, the results must show that in at least 95 percent of all such cases the difference is not due to chance; that the null hypothesis is wrong 95 percent of the time. Put another way, a researcher will not conclude that the research hypothesis is supported unless the statistical test shows that there is only a 5 percent chance or less that a Type I error is being committed. If the chances of a Type I error are 5 percent or less, the findings are said to be *"statistically significant."* If the results are not statistically significant, one has produced adverse evidence concerning the theory. If they are significant, one goes on to the next step.

Establishing that a difference between two or more groups, or a relationship between two or more variables, is statistically significant is not the same as establishing its sociological significance. Statistical significance is essentially a function of two things: the extent of difference and the size of the sample. A very small difference between two categories with very large numbers of cases may be statistically significant, as might a very large difference among categories with small numbers of cases. The question is, how much difference does one need to find in order to claim support for a particular research hypothesis? Recall that almost all sociological propositions (hypotheses) are stochastic. Rarely, if ever, will one find that all units in one category behave in one way and all units in another behave in another. Typically, there will be a difference in degree: more of Class A does such-and-such than of Class B. How much of a difference between A and B must be found for one to say that the findings are meaningful? The third type of statistics, *measures of association* (e.g., Lambda, gamma, R^2), *are designed to tell us how much of the variation in the dependent variable is accounted for (explained) by changes in the independent variable.* In a very large sample, the relationship between two variables may be statistically significant, but as little as 1 or 2 percent of the total variation of the dependent variable may be explained by the independent. Is that finding sociologically meaningful?

Statistics cannot finally answer the question of whether the research hypothesis has been supported. If the findings are not statistically significant, then the research hypothesis has been disconfirmed. But when the findings are statistically significant, the sociologist must finally determine whether the amount of variance explained constitutes "enough" to say that the hypothesis is supported by the data. The statistics do not speak for themselves; they require interpretation by the human mind. One final note of caution is appropriate. Just as different ways of phrasing questions and/or answers can yield different results, different statistics sometimes lead to different conclusions. Only a thorough knowledge of statistics can help one to interpret the statistical evidence and reach decisions concerning whether or not the data support the hypothesis, and even then there may be no one final answer. Again, the educated discretion of the scientist cannot be replaced.

No statistic provides an explanation. Statistics can tell us that a relationship probably exists (tests of significance) and how strong that relationship is (measures of association). Statistics can also be used to control for the effects of other variables. *Statistical control refers to procedures* (e.g., partial correlation) *which allow one to estimate the effects of one variable independently of the effects of other variables.* It allows one to examine relationships between some variables while holding the effects of others constant. Statistical control is thus a rough equivalent to the actual control which can be exercised in a laboratory setting.

Recall that a relationship found between two variables may be spurious, that is, they may both be affected by a third variable which provides the real linkage between the variables in question. The three types of statistics discussed earlier will not tell the researcher that a relationship is or is not spurious. The scientist must choose a number of variables which she or he suspects (on the basis of her or his sociological knowledge) may be impacting the noted relationship. The researcher may then control these statistically. Stated in another way, one builds confidence that the test results support the theory by testing and rejecting as many alternative possibilities as possible. If one can disprove enough other possibilities, one can place more faith in the explanation offered for the relationship found. Thus, the simple test of the research hypothesis alone is often not a sufficient test of a theory. The ability to reject simultaneously other possible explanations of the phenomenon in question greatly enhances the conclusions that can be drawn from the test. The researcher must have been able to foresee these alternatives at the time the research instrument was developed, or the data needed to test them will not be available.

To exemplify this, let us suppose that we have a theory which attempts to explain why married women who are employed choose to have a smaller number of children than those who are not gainfully employed. The theory claims that this happens because the satisfactions employed women receive from work are greater than those they would receive from having additional children who, in turn, would interfere with their jobs. The logical corollary of this might be that married women who are satisfied with their jobs have fewer children than employed married women who are not job-satisfied. Let us suppose that we find that employed married women have a smaller average number of children than those not employed, and that the job-satisfied have yet a smaller average number than those who are not satisfied with their jobs. Further, let us suppose that these findings are statistically significant and that the differences between groups are large enough to be sociologically meaningful. We thus have evidence that might support our theory. There is reason to believe, however, that family income, type of job (or type of job one could get if employed), and education (among other things) are major factors explaining the number of children a woman desires, the decision to be or not to be gainfully employed, and the level of job satisfaction among the employed. If we controlled statistically the effects of these three new variables and still found the same relationships as originally, we would have rendered unlikely three major alternative explanations and could place more faith in our original formulation. Of course, it is possible that our original formulation was not wrong, only incomplete, and that some or all of the other three variables are also important. Statistical control would help us to discover this too.

What can research findings tell us about a theory? They can tell us that the theory, as stated, is probably wrong. If one can assume that there were no important errors made in the research process, the data can disconfirm a theory. If findings emerge which conform to the relationships specified in the hypotheses, if those findings are statistically as well as sociologically significant, and if major alternative explanations can be ruled out, then one can claim to have found support for the theory. Depending on the nature of the sample (i.e., the scope of the population on which the theory has been tested), the degree to which the measurements of the variables are valid indicators of the theoretical concepts, and the extent of articulation between the research design and the theoretical explanation, one can reach conclusions about how extensive the support is for the theory. However, given the possibility that another test may fail to support the theory, one can never say a given theory has been proven.

D. REVISING THEORIES

The number of hypotheses examined in a given test of a theory will typically be fairly large. Moreover, the number of alternative explanations examined may be substantial. In all likelihood, at least some findings will emerge which do not conform to the theory as stated. They may contradict parts of the theory and/or they may point up important variables omitted from the theory. One can choose simply to toss out the theory and start over. This is very radical surgery and should be done only when key propositions are disconfirmed. In fact, given the emphasis on preventing Type I errors and, therefore, the relatively high probability of committing Type II errors, one would probably not reject a total theory on the basis of only one test. This is especially so if the findings are in the direction suggested by the hypotheses but fail to reach statistical significance. If several tests demonstrate that a number of important components of the theory are incorrect, then it becomes fruitful to reject the theory and begin anew. Most often a more gradual process of theory revision occurs. Only much later, when a new theory is developed which does a better job of explaining the known facts, is the revised theory rejected. Let us examine briefly an exercise in theory revision.

Let us suppose that we have tested an hypothesis derived from the proposition "the more people from two groups interact with one another, the less prejudiced the attitudes of each group's members toward the other group become." In our hypothetical test the prejudicial attitudes of blacks and whites toward one another were measured, and subsequently members of both racial groups were assigned to each of four groups, a control group and three experimental groups. Experimental Group I members were seated in a room and told simply to talk and get to know each other. Group II was given a task and told that each person's contribution to the solution of the task would be graded, the grades would be curved, and the grade earned by the individual would be the basis for how much money was paid to that person. Group III members were also given a task and told that, depending on how quickly the group as a whole completed that task, all members would share equally in a monetary reward. The control group did not do anything and members were prohibited from communicating with one another. The members of the four groups were subsequently retested on their racial prejudices.

Let us suppose that the findings were as follows: the control group experienced no attitude change; Experimental Group I experienced no statistically significant change; Group II showed more prejudice after their experience, while Group III manifested less prejudice in the after-test. Changes in both Groups II and III were statistically and sociologically significant. Thus, in one circumstance interaction failed to change prejudicial attitudes; in one it increased and in one it decreased such attitudes. Clearly, our original proposition is inadequate as stated. It can be revised, however, to account for the findings: "The more people from two groups interact in pursuit of a common goal (Group III), the less prejudiced the attitudes of each group's members toward the other group become," and "the more people from two groups interact competitively (Group II), the more prejudiced the attitudes of each group's members toward the other group become."

Let us further suppose that we controlled for the effects of sex on these relationships and found that among females scores in Experimental Group I changed (prejudice was reduced) as well as Groups II and III (in the directions specified above). Among males, scores changed only in Groups II and III. This finding necessitates further revisions: "Among females, the more people from two groups interact in situations that are not competitive (Groups I and III), the less prejudiced the attitudes of each group's members toward the other group become"; "Among males and females, the more two groups interact in competitive situations (Group II), the more prejudiced the attitudes of each group's members toward the other group become"; and "Among males, the more two groups interact in cooperative situations (Group III), the less prejudiced the attitudes of each group's members toward the other group become."

Thus, the findings are used, via a process of induction, to change, enlarge upon, refine the theoretical propositions. New propositions may be added to account for the data, and/or old propositions may be reworded to include contingencies, exceptions, "givens," additional independent and/or intervening variables, and so on. The next step would be a return to the empirical world for a test of the revised proposition(s), and so on in a process that has no end.

E. EXEMPLAR

The Exemplar theory has not been systematically tested to date. In the original formulation (Chafetz, Dworkin and Dworkin, 1976) exemplary cases (females, blacks, Mexican-Americans, and Japanese-Americans) were presented for one historical era (the years preceding, including, and immediately following World War II) in one nation (the United States). Examples, however, do not constitute a test of a theory. Typically (as is our case), one selects examples precisely because they support the basic elements of the theory being presented. They thus constitute a very biased sample of the population to which the theory presumably applies. In order to test the theory, a sample of cases needs to be selected that has not been prescreened, a sample which includes cases in which a probability exists that evidence adverse to the theory could be found. In other words, some form of random sampling needs to be employed.

In order to test the theory, a research and sampling design would need to be created. Possible operationalizations for the variables were already discussed in Chapter 4. The substance of the theory concerns change over time in the occupational characteristics (the two dependent variables) and related phenomena (the intervening variables) of large categories of the population of a society as well as changes in general socioeconomic conditions of the society as a whole (the independent variables). Of necessity, the research design would be of a longitudinal type. The same groups within a given society would be examined in terms of the relevant variables during a period extending over a decade or more.

The sample would have to take into account the scope of the theory, which has not previously been specified. Is the theory relevant to the United States only? To industrial societies? To all societies? For now, let us say that the scope is all industrial societies. Thus, one major sampling task is to select a number of different industrial societies. Another sampling task refers to time, or the selection of historical periods to study. One could, for instance, break the post-Industrial Revolution history of each society in the sample into decades (or twenty-year periods, etc.) and randomly select a number of these time units for study. Or, one could use established historical units, such as the era between the two World Wars. Finally, the dominant social majorities of each society must be defined, and all social minorities in each society in each time unit sampled must be identified. The social majorities would have to be studied in each time period and each society in the sample. There would need to be a method of randomly selecting a number of social minorities to comprise the sample. In short, a full test of the theory would involve sampling societies, times, and minority groups randomly. Given the large number of variables, the difficulties in accumulating all the types of data necessary, and other practical problems, it is highly unlikely that one could indeed test this theory on such a broad sample in any one research project. A number of tests would, therefore, be required to begin to place faith in the theory, if indeed, the findings in the first few warranted further testing.

It is, of course, not possible to discuss data analysis and theory revision in the absence of research findings. However, even in the process of researching a few selected examples one finding emerged which necessitates a revision of our theory. At least some of the minority groups examined for the World War II era should have mounted social movements, according to our theory. None did at that time. It is obvious (in retrospect) that during a widely supported war effort, the emergence of a social movement on behalf of minority rights would have been viewed as "unpatriotic" and treated harshly. Clearly, our theory needs to be restated to stipulate that social movements on behalf of minority groups will tend not to arise during periods defined popularly (e.g., like World War II but unlike the Viet Nam War) as national emergencies, even when the other conditions necessary to their emergence are present. Undoubtedly, a test of the theory would reveal many other necessary revisions.

With this, the discussion of the exemplar theory is concluded. In the next chapter, criteria for evaluating theories will be discussed. After reading the concluding chapter, you may wish to try your hand at a complete evaluation of our theory in terms of the criteria discussed.

STUDENT EXERCISES

1. Choose at least three propositions from the exercises you did in the last

chapter (Chapter 6). First, for each concept in each proposition specify at least three possible operationalizations. What, if any, are the problems of validity involved? Next, write at least three hypotheses for each proposition. If you wished to test the hypotheses derived from each of the three propositions, what kind of research design(s) would be best? Why? Who (or what) would you sample? Why? What means would you use to collect your data? Why?

2. Do the same exercises as in Number 1 for both of the following (i.e., create three variables for each concept, write at least three hypotheses, propose a research design, specify who or what is to be sampled and how the data would be collected, and justify all parts of your answer):

   a. The higher their social status, the greater the tendency of people to support the status quo.
   b. The more complex the social system, the greater the probability of internal conflict.

CHAPTER **8**

Concluding Remarks

The first seven chapters of this primer were designed to instruct you in the importance of theory development, the basic techniques used in creating theories, and some of the fundamental issues and problems involved in developing and testing theories. Many of the techniques, problems, and issues discussed are not unique to creating and testing theories in sociology. They pertain to research engaged in for reasons other than theory testing and to disciplines other than sociology. More crucially, they pertain to thinking more clearly and precisely in every aspect of life. In this, the concluding chapter, material from the previous chapters will be brought together in a brief discussion of the criteria by which theories may be evaluated and in an overview of the joys and sorrows of the intellectual enterprise we call science.

A. CRITERIA FOR EVALUATING THEORIES

At the outset of this book "theory" was defined as consisting of "a series of relatively abstract and general statements which collectively purport to explain some aspect of the empirical world." Subsequently, the elements which comprise theories were delineated: assumptions, concepts (including classifications) and their definitions, and propositions. Throughout the book the point was also made that theories are not only statements about the empirical world, they are logical systems, too. Each of these points provides one or more criteria upon

113

which a given theory may be evaluated. The most important of these criteria may be summarized as follows:

1. Does the theory do a good job of accounting for (explaining) the known facts about the empirical phenomenon (a) in question? Stated in another way, are there a large number of relevant facts for which the theory cannot account which are thus anomalies for that particular theory? What, in short, is the theory's explanatory power?

2. Is the theory stated in such a way that it is readily amenable to empirical test? Stated otherwise, is the theory falsifiable through research?

3. Are the assumptions clearly delineated?

4. Whether the assumptions are explicitly stated or implicit, are they "reasonable" ones to make?

5. Are the concepts carefully defined and used in a manner consistent with their definitions? Are they unidimensional? Are classifications (if any) logically coherent and in conformity with the rules of mutual exclusiveness and all-inclusiveness?

6. Does the list of concepts include any which are minimum terms, or does the theory reduce the subject matter to that of another discipline by employing only borrowed terms?

7. Does it appear possible to create valid operationalizations for the major concepts in the theiry?

8. Does the explanation provided by the theory avoid tautology?

9. Does the explanation provided by the theory separate causes from consequences and thereby avoid teleology?

10. How precisely is the nature of the explanation(s) spelled out? In other words, are the linkages between concepts ambiguous or clearly delineated?

11. How parsimonious is the statement of the theory, especially the list of propositions?

12. Is the logic within the theory consistent, or are there internal contradictions?

In addition to these criteria, which flow from the discussion of the elements involved in theory construction and the definition of "theory" per se, a theory may be evaluated in terms of some other issues. Is the subject matter of the theory "trivial," "common-sensical," or does it provide important or interesting new insights? How broad a scope does the theory cover? Another way to say this is to ask if the theory is general (universal) or does it apply to (relatively) unique phenomena in time

114

(historically) and/or space (geographically)? Generally, the broader the scope, the more important the theory. Related to this is the issue of abstractness: how abstract are the concepts employed in the theory? Generally, as long as the theory remains testable, the more abstract the concepts, the broader the scope and, therefore, the more important the theory. Another issue concerns whether or not the theory is consistent with other theories widely accepted in the discipline (although aimed at explaining different phenomena). Are the implications of the theory contradictory to those of other theories? If they are contradictory, what is the evidence that the theory in question is superior to the others? Finally, without forgetting the contingent and stochastic nature of sociological explanations, it is, nonetheless, legitimate to ask to what extent the theory is capable of generating predictions that research later supports.

On the basis of these criteria, few if any sociological theories can be said to approach the ideal. In evaluating theories the real issue is how close they come to conforming to the canons of "good theory," not whether or not they conform perfectly to all the rules. These criteria for evaluation are useful for two purposes. First, one may often improve a theory by evaluating its weaknesses and striving to correct those to conform better to the canons set forth. Second, if there are two or more competing theories which purport to explain the same phenomenon(a), one can use these criteria to identify one as "better" than the other(s) and, on that basis, choose to employ it rather than its rival(s).

It should be noted that, while one may assess a theory on many of the criteria knowing nothing but that theory, a full assessment requires extensive knowledge of the literature concerning the specific area of study. For instance, if one were evaluating the exemplar theory, one could, knowing nothing about minorities or labor force statistics, determine whether or not the theory is teleological, tautological, parsimonious, and logically consistent, whether the assumptions are carefully delineated, the concepts adequately defined and consistently employed, the linkages carefully spelled out, and so on. One could not, however, judge to what extent the known facts are accounted for or whether or not the theory in question is compatible with (or contradictory to) other theories in sociology. As pointed out in Chapter 1, there is no substitute for reading the literature of a discipline. No less in the process of evaluating theories than in creating them, one must do one's "homework."

115

B. On the Joys and Sorrows of Doing Science

A science is any discipline which seeks to discover and explain regularities in some aspect of the empirical world. Given this definition, all sciences involve the related processes of research (i.e., discovery) and theory development (i.e., explanation). Regardless of the particular methods employed, or the aspect of the empirical world delineated as the province of a particular science (e.g., rocks, social interaction, the economy, atomic and subatomic particles), scientists are all involved in the same fundamental processes and share the same types of joys and sorrows, frustrations, and elations.

All scientists spend their lives, from the beginning of their training to the end of their career, learning what others, past and present, have learned about their subject matter. In short, there is always "homework" to be done. Moreover, given the burgeoning quantity of scientific output in this century (most scientists who have ever lived are alive and working today!), the burden of keeping up with the literature has assumed massive proportions. For that reason, if for no other, doing science for a serious scholar is rarely a forty-hour workweek. For that reason also, the subject areas about which scientists are expert become more and more narrow, more and more specialized, as each year passes. It is simply no longer possible to keep abreast of the literature in more than one or two specialty areas within one science at one time.

All scientists know that, regardless of the nature of their discovery or the brilliance of their theoretical contribution, it is destined to be surpassed eventually. We have seen that theories are constantly revised to conform better to the knowledge accumulated. Sooner or later a theory can no longer be "stretched" to account for newly discovered facts. A new theory is developed which accounts for the facts explained by the old plus those which were anomalies under the old. The new theory gradually comes to replace the old, which in turn takes its place in the history books of that science but is removed from its textbooks. Paradigms experience the same destiny, although they may last for a longer period of time before being superseded. How quickly a new theory or paradigm replaces an old is, as Kuhn pointed out (1962), related to such nonrational forces as the politics and prestige structure of a discipline, but sooner or later the old will be replaced. In short, science is a never-ending process and the facts, theories and paradigms of today are destined to become the historical curiosities of tomorrow.

But most scientists do not make brilliant discoveries or create major

116

theoretical breakthroughs. They are destined to make more modest contributions in relative obscurity. Their contributions are, however, collectively of major importance. They provide the basis upon which the brilliant and/or "lucky" few will create their more obvious and famous breakthroughs. The facts carefully accumulated by hundreds of obscure scientists constitute the "homework" for that relatively rare individual who will put them together in a new way.

These are humbling thoughts. When we add the facts that a scientist can never legitimately claim to have finally "proven" anything, that years of painstaking research often do not even provide clear answers of support or disconfirmation of a given proposition, the frustrations involved in doing science are clear.

All sciences involve conformity to rules regarding how facts are to be accumulated, analyzed, and generalized. This primer has involved a discussion of many such rules in sociology. However, doing science is never a cookbook exercise; it is never simply a matter of conforming to a series of steps (a "recipe") leading to a scientific finding or discovery. Nor does the existence of high-speed computing machinery alter the fundamental nature of doing science, since computers are only capable of doing that which human beings ask them and instruct them to do. At every stage of theory building and research imagination and creativity play major roles. Whether one is framing a research problem, planning out a research or sampling design, creating a research instrument, figuring out what the data mean, defining a concept, or creating a proposition, no automatic procedures exist that replace a hardworking, well-educated, creative human mind. These are the attributes which C. Wright Mills (1959) called the "sociological imagination" and saw as a way of life, not simply a method of work. He said about the process of reflection involved in exercising the sociological imagination that "on those rare occasions when it is more or less successful, [it is] the most passionate endeavor of which the human being is capable" (1959, p. 51).

For those who do science the joys come from knowing that one has done one's work with care and skill, as a craftsperson. They come from the process of exercising one's creativity, imagination, and intelligence in a relatively independent, unsupervised work environment. Few joys surpass the experience of seeing, for the first time, something one has created in print with one's own name attached to it (and few sorrows surpass the rejection of one's work by a publisher or editor). Joy is going to a professional meeting and hearing a colleague tell you that some piece of your work is important; it is receiving a letter from a colleague congratulating you on a paper or book you have written (never mind that it will be out-of-date or out-of-print in two years). It is knowing that your work may contribute to the solution of a problem that is plaguing your society or the world.

In short, scientists receive two types of satisfactions. There are those that arise internally when one has done one's work well, contributed something to the science, answered a nagging question or problem, satisfied in a small, perhaps temporary way one's intellectual curiosity. These joys depend upon having the type of personality and values which define these feelings as highly rewarding. The other source of satisfaction is external. It arises as a response to admiration given by others whom one respects as professional colleagues. Occasionally, one may also reap the praises of the public or public officials if one has provided an answer to a pressing practical problem. Few human beings fail to find joy in praise from others, especially others respected as knowledgeable.

Relative to other professions which require extensive postgraduate education, most scientists are not highly paid. To persevere in science requires that a person value the intellectual enterprise in its own right. Without that, the frustrations are too many, the rewards too few for a lifetime of hard work. With that value, the process of doing science is fun; it is its own reward. If the product is substantial (e.g., a major discovery is made), that is a delightful bonus. We are an intellectually questing species. In everyday life we "theorize" constantly about our world and the people who populate it. Scientists, including sociologists, pay the costs and reap the rewards from making a vocation and life commitment of that which, for most people, is an avocation.

STUDENT EXERCISES

1. In Chapter 1, Exercise 5, you either selected someone else's theory or began to create your own to explain something of interest to you within sociology. In Chapter 6, Exercise 3, you rendered that theory in propositional form. Now, using the criteria for evaluating theories presented in this chapter, evaluate and, if possible, improve the theory with which you have been working.

Postscript to Teachers

I have found in teaching sociological theory that the material covered in this primer (which I teach as Unit I in the course) comes "alive" for students if they are later asked to apply it (on take-home exams and/or in term papers) to the ideas of the classical theorists they study. Thus, a student would take one of the theories developed by such thinkers as Marx, Durkheim, or Pareto and: (1) carefully define a series of central concepts; (2) spell out the implicit and explicit assumptions underlying the theory; (3) develop several propositions that collectively express the theory and utilize the major concepts listed in Step 1 above; (4) explain which are the independent, dependent, and intervening variables in their propositions; (5) explain the nature of the linkages within each proposition; (6) attempt to develop operational definitions and a general plan to test the theory empirically; and (7) discuss the problems they had in converting the theory, as presented originally, into this format, including any deficiencies noted in the original version.

Another exercise which helps students to practice the various steps in theory construction consists of the following. Give students a list of about five concepts which generally relate to some one phenomenon (i.e., at least one could be a dependent variable and the others could be treated as independent and/or intervening variables) *or* allow students to choose their own set of concepts. The student is then required to: (1) define the concepts; (2) state a series of propositions which, collectively, employ all concepts on the list and add up finally to an explanation of one of them; (3) delineate which are the independent, dependent and intervening variables in each proposition; (4) explain the nature of the

119

linkages within each proposition; and (5) attempt to develop operational definitions and a general plan to test the theory empirically.

A final word concerns the exemplar used throughout this primer. It has been purposely set off in its own sections, and is only rarely discussed outside of those sections. It was included not only to exemplify the points made in each chapter but also to try to convey some of the excitement and struggle involved in the (still far from completed) process of developing a new theory. It may prove to involve too many variables to be readily comprehensible by some students. For this reason, and because it is neither a completed theory, a tested theory, nor a standard theory in the field, you may wish to substitute your own or one of the classic theoretical formulations and omit the Exemplar sections. The omission of the Exemplar sections from the reading of this primer should in no way detract from students' ability to understand the text.

References

CHAPTER 1

Chafetz, J.S., R.J. Dworkin, and A.G. Dworkin. 1976. New migrants to the rat race: a model of rates of labor force participation and patterns of occupational deployment by gender, race and ethnicity. Unpublished manuscript.

Merton, R.K. 1957. *Social theory and social structure*. Glencoe, Ill.: The Free Press.

CHAPTER 2

Bendix, R. and S.M. Lipset. 1964. *Social mobility in industrial society*. Berkeley, Calif.: University of California Press.

Chafetz, J.S., R.J. Dworkin, and A.G. Dworkin. 1976. New migrants to the rat race: a model of rates of labor force participation and patterns of occupational deployment by gender, race and ethnicity. Unpublished manuscript.

Durkheim, E. 1893. *The division of labor in society*. trans. G. Simpson. Glencoe, Ill.: The Free Press, 1947.

Lenski, G. 1966. *Power and privilege: a theory of social stratification*. New York: McGraw-Hill.

Merton, R.K. 1957. *Social theory and social structure*. Glencoe, Ill.: The Free Press.

Parsons, T. 1951. *The Social System*. Glencoe, Ill.: The Free Press.

Timasheff, N.S. 1959. "Order, causality and conjuncture," in *Symposium on sociological theory*, ed. L. Gross, pp. 145-166. New York: Harper and Row.

CHAPTER 3

Durkheim, E. 1897. *Suicide*. trans. J.A. Spaulding and G. Simpson. Glencoe, Ill.: The Free Press. 1951.

REFERENCES

Gouldner, A. 1970. *The coming crisis of western sociology*. New York: Avon Books.
Kuhn, T. 1962. *The structure of scientific revolutions*. Chicago: University of Chicago Press.
Lenski, G. 1966. *Power and privilege: a theory of social stratification*. New York: McGraw-Hill.
Ritzer, G. 1975. *Sociology: a multiple paradigm science*. Boston: Allyn and Bacon.
Thomas, W.I. 1923. *The unadjusted girl*. Boston: Little, Brown.

CHAPTER 4

Weber, M. 1947. *The theory of social and economic organization*. ed. and trans. T. Parsons. New York: The Free Press.
Zetterberg, H. 1965. *On theory and verification in sociology*. 3rd ed. Totowa, N.J.: Bedminster Press.

CHAPTER 5

Durkheim, E. 1893. *The division of labor in society*. trans. G. Simpson. Glencoe, Ill.: The Free Press.
Etzioni, A. 1964. *Modern organizations*. Englewood Cliffs, N.J.: Prentice-Hall.
Hage, J. 1972. *Techniques and problems of theory construction in sociology*. New York: John Wiley.
Kornhauser, W. 1959. *The politics of mass society*. Glencoe, Ill.: The Free Press.
Merton, R.K. 1957. *Social theory and social structure*. Glencoe, Ill.: The Free Press.
Petersen, W. 1958. A general typology of migration. *American Sociological Review*, 23:256-266.
Redfield, R. 1941. *The folk culture of Yucatan*. Chicago: University of Chicago Press.
Sorokin, P. 1937-41. *Social and cultural dynamics*. New York: American Book Co.
Tönnies, F. 1957. *Community and society*. trans. Charles P. Loomis. Lansing, Mich.: Michigan State University Press.
Weber, Max. 1949. *The methodology of the social sciences*. trans. E. Shils and H. Finch. Glencoe, Ill.: The Free Press.
———. 1958a. Characteristics of bureaucracy. In *From Max Weber: essays in sociology*, ed. H. Gerth and C.W. Mills, pp. 196-198. New York: Galaxy Books.
———. 1958b. *The Protestant ethic and the spirit of capitalism*. trans. T. Parsons. New York: Scribners.

CHAPTER 6

Bendix, R., and S.M. Lipset. 1964. *Social mobility in industrial society*. Berkeley, Calif.: University of California Press.
Lenski, G. 1966. *Power and privilege: a theory of social stratification*. New York: McGraw-Hill.

Zetterberg, H. 1965. *On theory and verification in sociology.* 3rd ed. Totowa, N.J.: Bedminster Press.

CHAPTER 7

Chafetz, J.S., R.J. Dworkin and A.G. Dworkin. 1976. New migrants to the rat race: a model of rates of labor force participation and patterns of occupational deployment by gender, race and ethnicity. Unpublished manuscript.

Webb, E., D. Campbell, R. Schwartz and L. Sechrest. 1966. *Unobtrusive measures: non-reactive research in the social sciences.* Chicago: Rand McNally.

Zetterberg, H. 1965. *On theory and verification in sociology.* 3rd ed. Totowa, N.J.: Bedminster Press.

CHAPTER 8

Kuhn, T. 1962. *The structure of scientific revolutions.* Chicago: University of Chicago Press.

Mills, C. W. 1959. On intellectual craftsmanship. In *Symposium on Sociological Theory,* ed. L. Gross, pp. 25-53. New York: Harper and Row.

Glossary

All-inclusiveness, principle of: In classification schemes and operationalized variables of all types, the requirement that there must be a category or value to accommodate every possible case in the real world. (p. 66)

Aristotelian definitions: Verbal definitions comprised of two parts: the first, *genus proximum,* tells what the phenomenon in question has in common with a larger class of phenomena; the second, *genus specifica,* tells what is peculiar to the phenomenon in question. (p. 49)

Assumptions: Statements taken as given and not subject to direct empirical testing. (p. 33)

Axiom: The basic propositions in an axiomatic theory; synonym for "postulate." (p. 83)

Axiomatic theory: The most parsimonious means of presenting a theory; the number of propositions is reduced to only those necessary to derive all other propositions logically. (p. 83)

Borrowed terms: Primitive terms which were taken over from another discipline. (p. 52)

Causality: The assumption that there is a logical connection between perceivable events, processes, and other phenomena through which an action by one element brings about an action by another or others. (p 35)

Classification: See "multidimensional concepts."

Classification scheme: A variable which has as its values multidimensional concepts. (p. 66)

Closed systems: A system which includes all variables needed to explain change in any of the constituent parts; opposite of "open systems." (p. 23)

Coextensive linkage: In a proposition, a linkage that conveys no time dimension; the simultaneity of the variables involved; opposite of "sequential linkage." (p. 77)

Concepts: Words which are at least relatively abstract and which comprise the building blocks or basic content of sociological theories. (p. 45)

Conjuncture: The interaction between phenomena or causal chains in concrete space and time. (p. 21)

Constant: Something that cannot take on different values; opposite of a "variable." (p. 53)

Constructed type: A type based on a study of many examples of a phenomenon in which the attributes listed represent those most often found empirically. (p. 70 and 71)

Contingent linkage: In a proposition a linkage that conveys that the result occurs only if the original input plus something else occurs; opposite of "sufficient linkage." (p. 77)

Correlation coefficient: A statistic that tells us to what extent and in what way two variables are related in a linear fashion to one another; see "direct relationship" and "inverse relationship." (p. 15)

Cross-sectional design: A type of research design in which subjects are studied at only one point in time and various subgroups within the total sample are compared to one another, or the relationships between different variables, as they are distributed within the sample, are examined. (p. 97)

Data analysis: The use of a variety of types of statistics to aid in deciding whether and to what extent the facts support the hypotheses being tested . (p. 103)

Deductive logic: Reasoning from the general or abstract to the specific or concrete; opposite of "inductive logic." (p. 7)

Dependent variable: That which is being explained by other variables in a theory, proposition or hypothesis. (p. 80)

Derived terms: Extralogical terms which are defined by reference to primitive terms in a theory. (p. 51)

Descriptive statistics: Those statistics which tell something about the characteristics of a sample or subsample. (p. 103)

Determinism: The assumption that an occurrence is amenable, at least

126

potentially, to causal explanation which cites the factors which predispose the activity or action in question. (p. 36)

Deterministic linkage: In a proposition a linkage which conveys that something will always occur if something else does; opposite of "stochastic linkage." (p. 77)

Direct relationship: In a correlation coefficient, the pattern where as the value of one variable increases (or decreases) the value of the other variable increases (or decreases); opposite of "inverse relationship." (p. 15)

Domain assumption: Within a given science those assumptions specific to the subject matter of a theory. (p. 39)

Ecological fallacy: Drawing conclusions about individuals on the basis of aggregate (group) data. (p. 54 and 55)

Empirical world: Reality as it is known to us directly or indirectly through our senses. (p. 2)

Equilibrium: Within some systems a tendency toward self-correction; for alterations in a system to be met by counterchanges; synonym for "homeostasis." (p. 24)

Experimental design: A type of research design in which the researcher structures a laboratory situation such that the hypothesized causal (independent) variable is the only known relevant input into the situation. (p. 95)

Extralogical words: Words which provide the content for particular theories and thus tend to be specific to a given science or even theory. (p. 51)

Extrapolation: Taking a trend which can be documented to exist and "predicting" the future as a simple continuation of that trend. (p. 18)

Feedback: Refers to the fact that, in systems, not only does change in one variable give rise to change in the others, but in turn, the original variable is further changed in response to changes in the others. (p. 24)

Functional explanation: Answering the question "why?" by pointing to the system of which the variable in question is a part. (p. 25)

Games: Theory-based models of social behavior, interaction, etc., in which players assume roles bound by rules in order to learn experientially. (p. 11)

Homeostasis: See "equilibrium."

Hypothesis: A proposition relating two or more variables; used in research. (p. 92)

Ideal type: A type in which the defining attributes are thought to comprise the fundamental essence of the phenomenon in question. (p. 71)

Independent variable: A variable used to explain a dependent variable but which is not itself explained in the theory or proposition. (p. 80)

Inductive logic: Reasoning from the concrete or specific to the general or abstract; opposite of "deductive logic." (p. 7)

Interval level of measurement: The next-to-highest level of measurement; intervals between ranked values of a variable are equal but there is no absolute zero. (p. 56)

Intervening variable: Any variable which forms a link between the independent variable(s) and the dependent and without which the former is not related to the latter. (p. 80)

Inverse relationship: In a correlation coefficient, the pattern where as the value of one variable increases the value of the other decreases; opposite of "direct relationship." (p. 15)

Irreversible linkage: In a proposition, a linkage which conveys that one variable impacts the other, but not vice versa; opposite of "reversible linkage." (p. 77)

Latent consequences (functions): The unanticipated, often long-range results of an action; opposite of "manifest consequence." (p. 27)

Level of measurement: See: "nominal," "ordinal," "interval," and "ratio levels of measurement." (p. 55 and 56)

Logical words: Words used in all sciences which provide connectives within a theory. (p. 51)

Longitudinal design: A variant of a panel research design in which a study is conducted at several points in time, but each time the people studied are different. (p. 97)

Manifest consequences (functions): The anticipated results of an action; opposite of "latent consequence." (p. 27)

Measures of association: Statistics which tell us how much of the variation in the dependent variable is accounted for by changes in the independent variable. (p. 105)

Middle-range theory: Merton's idea that sociology ought to concentrate on the development of less general theories designed to explain smaller components of social reality and amenable to systematic testing. (p. 6)

Minimum terms: Primitive terms which are unique to a given science. (p. 52)

Multidimensional concepts: Concepts which incorporate a number of different variables or unidimensional concepts; synonym for "classifications." (p. 63)

Mutual exclusiveness, principle of: In classification schemes and operationalized variables of all types, the requirement that categories and values are defined such that each case in the real world fits in only one. (p. 66)

Necessary explanation: A type of explanation in which the elements listed must be present to bring about the result in question. Also, a type of linkage within propositions; opposite of "substitutable linkage." (p. 22, 78)

Necessary and sufficient explanation: The most complete type of causal explanation, including all the conditions needed to bring about a given result; whenever those conditions are present that result will occur, but it will not occur in their absence. (p. 22)

Nominal level of measurement: The lowest level of measurement; the values taken by a variable are different but cannot be rank ordered. (p. 56)

Null hypothesis: Used in statistics, the hypothesis that states that no relationship exists between variables. (p. 104)

Open systems: A system in which other unknown or unspecified variables influence those which are defined as constituting the system; opposite of "closed system." (p. 23 and 24)

Operational definition: Defining a variable in terms of how it is measured. (p. 53)

Ordinal level of measurement: The second lowest level of measurement; the values of a variable can be ranked but the intervals between rankings cannot be assumed to be equal. (p. 56)

Ostensive definition: A definition which demonstrates the meaning of a word in a nonverbal fashion; opposite of "verbal definition." (p. 49)

Panel design: A research design in which the same people are repeatedly subject to the same "test" over time. (p. 96)

Paradigm: General orientation toward a subject matter based on assumptions concerning the nature of the reality in question, what questions are important to ask of that reality, and how best to attempt to answer those questions. (p. 36)

Parsimony: The brief, concise, and succinct statement of a theory. (p. 81)

Polar types: Two types which are considered the opposite of one another. (p. 70)

Population: All cases which fit a set of specifications. (p. 98)

129

Postulate: See "axiom."

Prediction: A statement about the future rooted in a comprehension of the reasons behind past occurrence of the same phenomenon; based on understanding (theory) of why observed trends are as they are. (p. 19)

Primitive terms: Extralogical words which are defined in their own right in a theory. (p. 51)

Proposition: A statement which asserts something about reality by stating a relationship between (linking) two or more theoretical concepts. (p. 75)

Random: The lack of pattern, order, or regularity in the occurrence of some phenomenon. (p. 35)

Random sampling: Selection of a sample in such a way that every unit in a population has an equal chance of being selected; lack of sampling bias. (p. 99)

Ratio level of measurement: The highest level of measurement; intervals between ranked values are equal, and a real or absolute zero exists. (p. 57)

Reductionism: In sociology, the use of nonsocial variables (e.g., biological or psychological) to explain social phenomena. (p. 38)

Reification: Treating abstractions as if they were real things. (p. 48)

Reliability: The stable functioning of a research instrument. (p. 57)

Research design: A general strategy or master plan for conducting a piece of research. (p. 95)

Research instrument: The sum total of all the operationalizations in a given research project. (p. 100)

Residual category: A value added to a variable or classification scheme which includes all cases not included under the named categories. (p. 66)

Reversible linkages: In a proposition, a linkage which conveys that each variable impacts the other; opposite of "irreversible linkage." (p. 77)

Sample: That part of the population actually studied in a given piece of research. (p. 98)

Science: Any discipline which seeks to discover and explain regularities in some aspect of the empirical world. (p. 116)

Scientific law: A proposition that has been repeatedly tested and supported by data and is therefore accepted as "true" by the scientific community. (p. 75)

Scientific revolution: Kuhn's term for those points in the history of a science when a new paradigm replaces a widely accepted old paradigm (p. 37)

Sequential linkage: In a proposition, a linkage which conveys a time dimension; that something must precede something else in time; opposite of "coextensive linkage." (p. 77)

Simulations: Theoretical models, often computerized, of real-life situations in which the values of different variables may be changed to note the results. (p. 10)

Spurious relationship: When an unknown third (fourth, fifth, etc.) variable is systematically related to the two in question and provides the real link between the phenomena in question. (p. 17)

Statistical control: Procedures which allow one to estimate the effects of one variable independently of the effects of other variables; rough equivalent to laboratory control. (p. 106)

Statistical significance: By convention, a probability of 5 percent or less that a Type I error is being committed in a given test of significance. (p. 105)

Stochastic: A synonym for probabilistic. Also, a type of linkage within a proposition; opposite of "deterministic linkage." (pp. 21, 77)

Substitutable linkage: In a proposition, a linkage that conveys that various alternatives may bring about (or result from) changes in another variable; opposite of "necessary linkage." (p. 78)

Sufficient explanation: One in which the elements listed will always bring about the result in question. Also, a type of linkage within propositions; opposite of "contingent linkage." (pp. 22, 77)

System: Any series of variables that is characterized by the fact that when change occurs in any one, the other variables tend to change in response. (p. 23)

Tautology: A statement that is true by definition; it cannot be falsified; circular reasoning. (p. 26)

Taxonomy: A classification scheme which is developed systematically by specifying a series of attributes and creating categories that exhaust the logical combinations of those attributes. (p. 67)

Teleology: An explanation which cites the result of something as its cause. (p. 26)

Tests of significance: Statistics which tell us the probability of a relationship, such as that which appears to exist between variables (or an apparent difference among groups) occurring by chance. (p. 104)

131

Theorems: Propositions which are derived logically from postulates (axioms) in axiomatic theory. (p. 83)

Theory: Theories consist of a series of relatively abstract and general statements which collectively purport to explain (answer the question "why?") some aspect of the empirical world. (p. 2)

Truth-asserting definitions: A verbal statement which purports to define a concept but which, in fact, is a hypothesis or proposition about some aspect of empirical reality; a definition which can be said to be true or false. (p. 50)

Type: A listing of attributes which collectively define a phenomenon; a methodological tool; see "ideal type," "constructed type" and "polar type." (p. 70)

Type I error: Rejecting a true null hypothesis, i.e., accepting as true a false research hypothesis. (p. 104)

Type II error: Failing to reject a false null hypothesis, i.e., rejecting a true research hypothesis. (p. 104)

Unidimensionality: Concepts and operationalizations which mean and measure only one dimension; opposite of "multidimensionality." (p. 54)

Validity: The degree to which what is being measured in a research endeavor corresponds to what the scientist thinks is being measured; the degree of correspondence between the operationalization and the theoretical concept. (p. 53)

Variable: Anything that can be measured empirically and can take on different values; opposite of a "constant." (p. 53)

Verbal definitions: All definitions which employ words; opposite of "ostensive definitions." (p. 49)

Verstehen: A method used within the social definitionist paradigm that stresses interpretive or empathic understanding of actors' motivations. (p. 39)

THE BOOK MANUFACTURE

Composition: Meridian Graphics, Incorporated
Chicago, Illinois
Printing and Binding: George Banta Company, Inc.
Menasha, Wisconsin
Internal and Cover Design: John Goetz
Type: Caledonia with Ultra Bodoni display